Thanks, Rich!
You've been a
great (support)
(Ke)

We appreciate all you do
for Outward Bound!
~ Sara Knol

On behalf of the entire
Outward Bound community,
thanks for being a
rock star! — Jason Michelson

Rich,
Thanks for going out and
attempting to get auction items.
It is so great to be able to
pass something to you and
know it will get done. I
hope you are ready for next
year! :)
   Thanks,
   Ashley

Rich,
Thanks so much.
You're a fantastic help!
— Christina

Outward Bound THE INWARD ODYSSEY volume 2

Photography
Mark Zelinski

Text

School Profiles	Rebecca Bear
Photo Captions	Mark Zelinski
Text Editor	Deanna Bean
Editorial Assistant	Andrew Nigel
Editorial Assistant	Jane George
Editorial Assistant	Claudia Kazmierczak

Millions have tasted the fruit of the seeds planted by Kurt Hahn more than 60 years ago. Many return from their Outward Bound experience to cultivate compassion and courage within their own communities. This book is dedicated to those who share that legacy.

Mark Zelinski

Published by:
From The Heart Publishing
119 Duncairn Crescent
Hamilton, Ontario, Canada L9C 6E9
Telephone: 905-630-2556
E mail: fromtheheart@interlog.com

Scans and digital imaging by Advantage Graphics International,
Hamilton, Ontario art@advantagegraphics.on.ca
Prepress assistance by Cesar Teves
Printed & Bound in Hong Kong, China by Book Art Inc., Toronto
Color Separator & Prepress by Rainbow Digicolor Inc; Toronto

ISBN 0-9685879-1-7

Cover and book design by Craig Ketchen, Pillar Design (www.pillar.cx)
and Mark Zelinski Photographic Design.

For information on the work of Mark Zelinski, purchasing books or use of photographs visit
www.MarkZelinski.com

Contents

BUCKINGHAM PALACE

When, in 1991, my father wrote the foreword to the first edition of Outward Bound: The Inward Odyssey, he did so from the unique perspective of one who had been a pupil of Kurt Hahn, the Headmaster of Gordonstoun school, who with Laurence Holt, of the Blue Funnel Line, had founded Outward Bound. Furthermore, he had been Patron of Outward Bound since 1953.

I cannot claim those qualifications, but my own life has been moulded by Kurt Hahn's influence, by his passion that education should give students the opportunity for self-discovery, the strength to deal with triumph and defeat, the willingness to accept responsibility and the imagination to question conformity.

From its small beginning in Aberdovey in North Wales in 1941, Outward Bound has spread worldwide. Kurt Hahn's philosophy is universally accepted, and yet the need for that self-confidence that will allow us to reach our full potential is greater than ever.

I hope that, in my turn, I will be able to use my experience of Kurt Hahn's philosophy at Gordonstoun, at Lakefield College School in Canada and later, in different circumstances, in the Royal Navy, to lead and support Outward Bound in the years ahead. We face big challenges and we will only surmount them by showing the imagination to adapt Hahn's original principles and the courage to weather the inevitable storms along the way.

If this new edition of Outward Bound: The Inward Odyssey is anything like its predecessor, it will serve to inspire future generations of leaders across the world.

HRH Prince Andrew

"I can't remember when I've worked so hard, had so much fun, or learned so much. I am learning to rid myself of petty fears and doubts. I am becoming conscious of my own strengths – both physical and mental. I feel a tremendous surge of spiritual growth as I realise for the first time in my life that I am capable, strong and good."

Outward Bound Participant

The publisher gratefully acknowledges the generous participation of these Canadian sponsors who made this book possible.

Dear Reader:

Camaraderie and challenge hold two very different definitions. You will find, however, that the Outward Bound movement makes camaraderie and challenge one and the same, awarding students with a new, exciting and well-earned sense of accomplishment and self-awakening.

This wonderfully vivid publication illustrates men and women from all walks of life, culture and of all ages becoming one to transcend challenge and adversity within nature's magnificent yet humbling environments.

Waterstick commends the Outward Bound team and their students for demonstrating to us all that seemingly insurmountable life-challenges can be met and overcome through unwavering camaraderie and determination.

Mark Lang
Mark Lang
General Manager, Waterstick Performance Paddles

Kara Holding Inc.

Mark Zelinski
Photographic Design

6

Joan Henderson

Phil Droznika

Norm Sutherland

Deanna Bean

Andrew Nigel

Cesar Teves

Jane George

Dear Reader,

Fox 40 International Inc. is proud to be participating in a book about such a dedicated program as that of Outward Bound. Taking part in this publication allows us to help raise awareness and promote the excellent opportunities found within this program.

Fox 40 whistles are used as key safety items within the Outward Bound training courses, which are conducted in over 30 countries worldwide. This directly assists our company in its global effort to the promotion of personal safety.

As a Hamilton, Ontario business, we are proud of the local community effort put forth to this international project. Outward Bound is an invaluable cause that touches many lives.

Sincerely,

Ron Foxcroft
President, Fox 40 International Inc.

The Inward Odyssey of Outward Bound by Dr. Anthony Richards

Outward Bound is an innovative, experience-based educational vision, the brain-child of its originator, Kurt Hahn, that has survived and flourished now for more than 60 years within the Outward Bound schools around the world. This is truly remarkable in a world where so many educational fads have come and gone in this time. Is it that the concept is so adaptable that it can be applied to many settings, or that the rationale and philosophy is timeless and has a universal appeal? The creator, Kurt Hahn, died in 1974, but his influence within Outward Bound and other educational initiatives is still very much alive.

Kurt Hahn was born in Germany in 1896, the son of a wealthy Jewish industrialist, but he lived much of his life in England. While he was still in high school in 1902, he spent a summer vacation in the Dolomites with friends from Abbotsholme, an English public school. It was during this trip, through discussions about the English public school system, that he first saw education as a potential tool for character-building of a special kind.

By 1904, his interest in education had grown into something of an obsession. It was at this time, while still a young man, that Hahn suffered severe sunstroke that left him with a disability over which he triumphed with the greatest courage. Turning adversity to opportunity, he took advantage of the long recovery periods associated with the sunstroke to study various educational philosophies in greater depth. It was from these studies that Hahn formulated the system of education that he promoted throughout his life. His system was strongly influenced by the insights of Plato, Baden Powell, Cecil Reddie, Dr. Arnold of Rugby, Herman Lietz and many others.

Inspired by this highly creative period of his life, one of Hahn's favorite aphorisms was "Your disability is your opportunity." He never missed a chance to pass on this idea to others.

It was his belief that every child is born with innate spiritual powers and ability to make correct judgments about moral issues. In the progression through adolescence, the child loses these spiritual powers and the ability to make moral judgments because of what Hahn called the diseased society and the impulses of adolescence. Hahn was acutely aware of social distresses. He described these as:

The decline in fitness due to the modern methods of locomotion.
The decline of initiative and enterprise due to the widespread disease of spectatoritis.
The decline of memory and imagination due to the confused restlessness of modern life.
The decline of skill and care due to the weakened tradition of craftsmanship.
The decline of self-discipline due to the ever-present availability of stimulants and tranquilisers.
The decline of compassion due to the unseemly haste with which modern life is conducted.

Kurt Hahn on his 80th birthday.

Hahn's goal was to provide an "ideal pasture" for a child's innate powers and abilities to manifest themselves. That ideal pasture became Outward Bound.

The creation of Outward Bound, as with many of Hahn's other accomplishments, was to some extent serendipitous.

War forced Hahn to return to Germany in 1914 where he first met and worked with Prince Max von Baden. The prince became his benefactor and together they started a school, based on Hahn's ideas: Schloss Salem. Salem became one of the most famous schools in Europe.

Later on, with the rise of Hitler in the early 1930s, and Hahn's outrage over Hitler's behaviour, Hahn was imprisoned in 1933, released through influential British connections and subsequently exiled to Britain. Because of his reputation for successful results, Hahn was invited to demonstrate the Salem educational system. Understanding all too well that the inertia of the established traditions of the English public school system would prove infertile ground for new ideas, he declined the offer.

Gordonstoun school.

Instead, he saw "fertile ground" in the northeast of Scotland, where he had convalesced while recovering from his sunstroke-related episodes. It was during those recovery periods that Hahn became friendly with the Cumming family. Later, this friendship bore fruit. The family made available the Gordonstoun Estate and in April, 1934, Hahn opened the now famous Gordonstoun School with two pupils. In September, they were joined by a third pupil, Prince Philip of Greece, who later became His Royal Highness the Duke of Edinburgh. (Prince Philip became the Patron of Outward Bound in 1953.)

By 1937, there was a full complement of about 150 students at Gordonstoun, and Hahn was looking for ways to make his system more accessible to the youth of the village. With this in mind, he created a three-part programme for young people to develop physical skills such as running, jumping and throwing; learn to live in the outdoors through an adventurous expedition; and embark upon a hobby or project. Completion of these activities to a prescribed standard earned the Moray Badge award (named after the school's home county of Morayshire).

It was not long before Hahn had ambitions to expand the Moray Badge programme to include more than a million young people. He recruited just the right man, James Hogan, an educator with similar ideals, to develop the County Badge, an adaptation of the Moray Badge, to the needs and culture of each county in England.

In the beginning, one of the counties was willing to adopt the programme provided a fourth component, service, was added. Hahn at first resisted. He said that it was not appropriate to give a badge for service. Compassion was an expectation of everyone. However, he had a change of heart and the County Badge programme was introduced to many counties in England in 1938. The concept of service became entrenched and has become a hallmark of Outward Bound ever since.

The four key elements to achieving the County Badge — which became an integral part of Outward Bound — are referred to as the "Four Pillars". These pillars are physical fitness; an expedition that provides challenge and adventure; a project that develops self-reliance and self-discipline; and, finally, a sense of compassion through service.

Between 1937 and 1940, there were several short residential courses offered to promote the County Badge. One of these was a 28-day introduction to the programme. Once introduced to the activities and required standards, participants were expected to complete the courses set before them during the following 12 months. They were then tested for the badge. During these short summer school programmes, Hahn felt that he was able to implant unforgettable memories in the minds of the students and create an enthusiasm amongst these boys for this special approach to learning. The 28-day immersion experience developed during these times was the inspiration for the future Outward Bound courses.

In 1940, Gordonstoun School was forced to evacuate its Scottish premises and set up in Plas Dinam, Wales, which was situated some forty kilometres from the coast. The distance from the ocean meant the loss of seamanship as an essential school activity. This pained Hahn deeply. As a result, he arranged to have boats sent down from Gordonstoun and moored at Aberdovey. Here, he rented an old boarding house so that students could undergo sea training.

At this point, Hahn had the idea of developing the short residential courses into ongoing training programmes. Meanwhile, Laurence Holt, part-owner of the Blue Funnel Shipping Company, was looking for a training programme for young sailors. Whereas older sailors were more likely to survive because of their formative experiences on sailing ships, Holt had found that the younger generation of sailors seemed to have lost the tenacity and fortitude needed to survive the rigours of war and shipwreck.

As James Hogan's tenure with the County Badge programme was coming to an end and Hahn wanted to keep him on, Hahn saw an opportunity to find the money to pay Hogan, to create an expansion of the school's courses, and to provide the training programme needed by Blue Funnel.

As Laurence Holt was interested in Hahn's ideas for ongoing courses, Hahn sent Hogan off to Liverpool to convince Holt that a training project was essential. Hogan made his presentation. After several retreats for private discussions, Holt finally returned to the meeting, struck the table, and made a short announcement:

"We'll (the Blue Funnel Shipping Company) support you. We'll give you one thousand pounds outright. We'll buy the house and put it at your disposal and we'll lend you, without charge, the trained men you need for the nautical side of your training. How will that do you?"

"Away lifeboat crew" at Aberdovey.

This was the birth of Outward Bound. Pushing forward, one of Holt's conditions was that the first course should begin on October 14, 1941, only five weeks after the offer was made! Once again, James Hogan came through and the Outward Bound school was established on the coast at Aberdovey where courses could be conducted on and around the sea.

Even though it was Hahn who had the original idea for the 28-day residential course, he disclaimed credit for Outward Bound. He often said that Laurence Holt was the real founder. Hahn will be better remembered as the "moving spirit" behind the Outward Bound movement. The name "Outward Bound" was offered by Holt because of the nautical connection. Hahn did not like the name and wanted to maintain the notion of the County Badge. It was not until much later that Hahn admitted that one of Outward Bound's greatest assets was its name.

In 1946, as a fundraising and administrative vehicle, Outward Bound Trust was established with the purpose of expanding the concept of Outward Bound and creating other schools. Other schools were indeed formed and today, more than 60 years later, there are 43 schools around the world.

The successes of Outward Bound to date, evident in the stories and photographs that follow, are a compelling tribute to the life and spirit of Kurt Hahn.

Hahn wanted to share this vision for a better world — and share it he did. From his vision, hundreds of thousands of young people around the world have become better and enriched people, and they in turn have helped others to share the same Outward Bound adventure.

Dr Anthony Richards is a retired professor from Dalhousie University, Nova Scotia. He completed his doctoral dissertation on Kurt Hahn in 1981 and has been a Hahn scholar ever since.

The Evolution of Outward Bound Year by Year

1941 · Hahn the dreamer, Holt the provider, and Hogan the facilitator establish the Aberdovey Sea School/Outward Bound Centre, which offers a 28-day residential course to demonstrate the efficacy of Hahn's County Badge ideas and provides for Holt's shipping companies a rapid training in survival after shipwreck. Bryneithyn, a grey stone house situated on a steep south-facing slope overlooking the Dovey Estuary, is purchased and adapted to its new role. Twenty-four boys enroll in the first course of the first Outward Bound Centre.

1943 · Jim Hogan resigns and is followed by Freddie Fuller, an experienced seaman and small-boat sailor, and an excellent teacher and inspirer of the young. He writes: "At this very period when the world was filled with fear and hatred, this time when for this country it was the very winter of a deadly war, this new enterprise and school was born, lifting like the wild spring flower from the cold earth, with new promise and new hope." And later: "The great strength of these early courses was team spirit and the growth of a sense of community. This was the contribution of Outward Bound to the survival at sea during the war. Before the war's end, there was the conviction that this had to be carried through to the days of peace. There was the realisation that the response of the boys attending at Aberdovey was much deeper than they had ever dreamed could develop."

1945 · World War II ends. Captain Fuller remembers sitting on the javelin field and having a discussion with Laurence Holt and one or two others about what should be done when the war is over: "[We] agreed that Outward Bound was based on sound principles and that with certain modifications it could be made to work as well for other young men as it had for our sailors. We thought that we could find young people in considerable numbers in service clubs, schools, the uniformed services, and in industry." In fact, the industrial apprentice system, a tradition going back to the 13th century, continued to be the method by which many lads received their on-the-job training. Since they would remain with their firms for several years in a situation of mutual loyalty, any experience that would make them healthier, more alert and therefore more productive would be as welcome to the sponsoring employers as to the participants. The logic proved irresistible and apprentices became the backbone of the British Outward Bound schools. Other recruits came from the armed forces, the police and the fire service. Within a few year, the training of these young men invariably included a month at Outward Bound.

1946 · The Outward Bound Trust is established, with an eye to expansion and to oversee fundraising, publicity and recruitment of staff and students. Its long-time chairman is Sir Spencer Summers, a Conservative MP, whose energy, enthusiasm and influence does a great deal to establish the Trust as an important and expanding force in British education.

The 1950s was the decade of Outward Bound expansion. Two mountain schools were established in England's Lake District, and two other U.K. centres were established hundreds of kilometres apart in Scotland and Devon. Josh Miner, who was to become the father of Outward Bound in the United States, came to meet Kurt Hahn and witness his work firsthand. And Outward Bound schools were opened on four continents, the products of Hahn's and the American-British Foundation of European Education's influence and the British Commonwealth network.

1950 · Eskdale, the U.K.'s first mountain school, opens in the Lake District; its first two wardens are mountaineers with international reputations. · Josh Miner makes his initial trip to Gordonstoun and other institutions overseen by Kurt Hahn. He is particularly impressed with the Gordonstoun School Final Report to Parents: "The student was rated on his public spirit, sense of justice, and ability to follow out what he believed to be the right course in the face of various physical and psychological obstacles; on ability to organise — both as shown in the doing of his work and his direction of younger boys; on ability to deal with the unexpected; and on his conscientiousness — both in everyday affairs and in tasks with which he was especially entrusted. His imagination and manners were evaluated, as were his manual dexterity, the quality of his handicraft and other practical work, and the quality of his work in music, drawing, and other artistic endeavours. His academic performance was also assessed. If he were a member of the Cliff Watchers, the Fire Service, or the Army or Sea Cadets, a service report was submitted by his command officer."

1951 · The first all-girls' courses are held at Eskdale.

1951-2 · Josh Miner teaches at Gordonstoun and becomes Director of Activities, which includes The Break: "Four mornings a

First Girls course at Eskdale, 1951

12

Climbing in the Allgänier Alps in Austria, Kurzchule Baad.

week, during a 50-minute break...each boy took part in two of a half-dozen events — sprinting or distance running, long or high jumping, discus or javelin throwing.... He competed only against himself, trying to better his previous best performance."

1952 • The Moray Sea School receives its official Outward Bound charter. • The Outward Bound Mountain School (East Africa) opens at Loitokitok on Mount Kilimanjaro. • Germany's first sea school at Weissenhaus is established; it eventually closes in the 1970s.

1953 • Kurt Hahn retires from Gordonstoun to pursue other educational interests, including the Atlantic College. • HRH the Duke of Edinburgh becomes Patron to Outward Bound.

1955 • Ullswater, a second U.K. mountain school set in the Lake District National Park, offers its first courses. • The Outward Bound School Lumut is established on Malaysia's west coast.

1956 • Germany's first mountain school at Baad, technically in Austria, is founded.

1958 • Outward Bound Australia begins running courses at Fisherman's Point, north of Sydney.

1959 • The Devon school opens in southwestern England on the banks of the River Dart; it closes in the 1970s.

The 1960s was the golden decade of Outward Bound. Two quite revolutionary programmes were set up in the U.K. Josh Miner's vow to bring Outward Bound to the United Sates was accomplished in just five years with many exciting applications. And seven more schools on four continents were added to the Outward Bound world directory.

1960 • The Netherlands opens a sea school, and it rapidly adapts to the times. • Hahn's first Atlantic College is established in Wales.

1961 • Zimbabwe's first Outward Bound school is called the Outward Bound Association of Central Africa and its mandate covers what is now Zimbabwe, Zambia and Malawi.

1962 • New Zealand's Cobham Outward Bound School is founded on the northeast corner of the nation's South Island. • Colorado Outward Bound School, set in the Rocky Mountains and the first in the Western Hemisphere, is founded and begins a U.S. tradition of involvement with inner-city youth that continues to this day.

1963 • The Outward Bound Trust of the U.K. authorises the use of the Outward Bound title in the U.S., which accords Colorado and subsequent U.S. schools official Outward Bound status. • Rhowniar, just north of Aberdovey, is purchased for the exclusive use of girls.

1964 • Zambia's Outward Bound Lake School in Mbala is created out of a coffee plantation and hotel near the southern end of Lake Tanganyika. • Minnesota's Outward Bound School, later called Voyageur, begins running courses on the Canadian border. • U.S. schools begin work with adjudicated youth.

1964-65 • Hurricane Island, a sea school off the coast of Maine, begins to operate.

1965 • The U.S. Outward Bound Board of Trustees sees its mission as twofold: to enter the mainstream of American education and life and to adopt the policy of Outreach, in Josh Miner's words, "to venture beyond itself to proselyte institutions capable of multiplying its influence." • The first all-women's courses in the U.S. begin at Voyageur. • Trenton, New Jersey's Action Bound programme sends 30 urban young people to Colorado, Minnesota, and Hurricane Island, the first step in an effective relationship between Action Bound and Outward Bound.

Hiking in New Zealand with the school and Queen Charlotte Sound in the distance.

14

1966 • The Massachusetts Division of Youth Services works closely with U.S. Outward Bound schools, with "statistically significant" results. • Northwest Outward Bound school, later Pacific Crest, begins running courses in the Northwest U.S.

1967 • City Challenge, a true Outward Bound revolution, is devised by Freddie Fuller, inspired by his work with American Peace Corps training. • The Outward Bound School Singapore is inaugurated on the island of Pulau Ubin, 15 kilometres from the city centre. • North Carolina Outward Bound establishes its base camp under Table Rock Mountain in the western part of the state. • Colorado Outward Bound and Denver East High School begin a far-reaching educational mainstream partnership.

1968 • Germany's second mountain school, at Berchtesgaden, is opened.

1969 • Outward Bound Western Canada, then known as OB British Columbia, begins operations in Keremeos, B.C. • The first co-educational courses in the U.S. begin at Voyageur. • The first co-educational courses in the U.K. begin at Rhowniar. • Dartmouth Centre is established at Dartmouth University in New Hampshire; it later closes. • Outward Bound meets Upward Bound at Wesleyan University in Connecticut, the successful start of a significant strand in the Outreach story of Outward Bound U.S.A. — one of the longest-running and most successful Outward Bound collaborations in which economically and culturally deprived ninth graders, identified as possessing college potential, experience firsthand a standard Outward Bound course at North Carolina. • Tom Price, a 30-year veteran of Outward Bound as instructor and warden on four continents, sums up the 1960s for the Outward Bound staff at that time: "To those of us who worked in the schools in those days, life felt rich. Work to us was like play to small children; the more serious and earnest it is, the greater the fun and excitement. Each course was like a little life-time of experience, and when it ended we were left deflated and drained, often with only a day or so before we had to wind up to the next."

In the 1970s, U.S. Outreach commitment begins to focus (and, in the 1990s, continues to focus) on three other major constituents: the urban disadvantaged through Urban Outward Bound bases (now) in Minneapolis/St. Paul, Chicago, Boston, Baltimore, Los Angeles, San Francisco, San Diego and Atlanta; industry, through the design and implementation of management training courses, based on need and demand; and the physically disabled and blind, substance abusers, victims of domestic violence, Vietnam veterans suffering from Post Traumatic Stress Disorder, academic underachievers, gifted high school students and recovering cancer patients.

This was also a period of cutbacks and retrenchment. Schools and centres were closed, moved and/or consolidated in both the U.K. and the U.S. Internationally, however, schools continued to open in North America, Asia, Africa and in Europe.

1970 • The Hong Kong Outward Bound School begins operations at its Tai Mong Tsai headquarters, situated on the north eastern tip of the New Territories. • The first winter courses are held in the U.S., at Voyageur Outward Bound School, heralding the advent of year-round operations. • Texas Outward Bound School, later Southwest Outward Bound, is established; but it subsequently closes.

1973 • Outward Bound Australia moves to the bush of the Australian Capital Territory; five years later, its permanent base is established nearby.

1975 · An Outward Bound centre is inaugurated in Lesotho, a country completely surrounded by the Republic of South Africa.

1976 · Loch Eil opens in the Scottish Highlands after the closure and "move" of the Moray Sea School. · Aberdovey and Rhowniar centres join forces, and Outward Bound Wales is formed. · The Canadian Outward Bound Wilderness School, the lone outpost on Black Sturgeon Lake in Northern Ontario, runs its first courses.

1977 · The Belgian Outward Bound School is founded.

1979 · The Outward Bound School Lumut in Malaysia moves its base to a more remote area. · Tanzanian Outward Bound Centre is opened on the southeastern slopes of Mount Kilimanjaro, due to the closure of the border between Kenya and Tanzania.

Perhaps the most radical directions Outward Bound took in the 1980s were realised in the two greatly diverse locations of New York City and New Zealand. The former established the first wholly urban centre, anticipating a new city-wilderness commitment by Outward Bound; the latter hosted the first international conference, a precursor and acknowledgment of the importance of a cohesive international movement.

1983 · New Zealand hosts the first international Outward Bound conference, celebrating the rebuilding of the centre at Anakiwa and 21 years in operation. · The Netherlands institutes its City Bound project.

1985 · The Outward Bound School Kinarut, Malaysia, opens on the island of Borneo after a three-year clearing and building project.

1986 · The Outward Bound School Lumut, Malaysia, is the site of the second international conference.

1987 · Outward Bound Zimbabwe is re-established after a ten-year hiatus due to the unstable political situation in the area. · Hors Limites Outward Bound France is founded, the first organisation to follow procedures for affiliate members formulated at the Malaysian conference. It later closes in the 1990s. · The New York City Outward Bound Center is established, the only independently chartered urban centre in the world. · The International Secretariat is formed, following the mandate of the second international conference.

1988 · Outward Bound Western Canada reorganises and moves to Pemberton, British Columbia. · Outward Bound Königsburg, Germany's new sea school, enrolls its first students at a site on the Baltic Sea. · The third international conference is held at Cooperstown, New York, resulting in the formation of an International Advisory Board with regional representation and in an internationally-agreed mission statement.

1989 · Outward Bound Japan becomes a reality after twenty years as a dream. · Harvard Graduate School of Education initiates a joint venture with Outward Bound U.S.A. over a three-year period to implant the Outward Bound experience-based teaching approach into public education in a variety of meaningful ways.

The pace of growth of Outward Bound countries more than doubled in the 1990s. Thirteen new countries received licenses to operate, compared with ten in the previous two decades combined! The 1990s decade may be characterised as invention and reinvention.

The old "war canoe" near Voyageur's Minnesota base circa 1980s.

Mark Zelinski presents the first copy of The Inward Odyssey to HRH Prince Philip in 1991 at Aberdovey.

The brigantine, Ji Fung, was sold in 2002, having served Outward Bound Hong Kong for 20 years.

1990 • New centres open in Czechoslovakia and Hungary. Following the 1993 political separation of the Czech and Slovak Republics, two separate centres were licensed, each of which have brings a creative approach to programme design using drama. Much of the development in Eastern Europe is supported by Outward Bound Germany through the opening of a new centre in the former East Germany at Schweriner See and in 1996 at Schloss Krochlendorff. • The Indonesian centre opens outside Jakarta. (This centre has continued to expand and thrive despite a most difficult political and economic situation.)

1991 • The fourth international conference is held at Aberdovey to celebrate the 50th anniversary of its opening.

1993 • A vigorous centre, focused on repairing the racial divide, opens in South Africa and experiences strong growth, while other centres in Africa struggle with identity and difficult economic conditions. • A centre in Romania is provisionally licensed.

1994 • In the United States, the Expeditionary Learning Outward Bound evolves out of collaboration with Harvard University. It proves to be one of the most successful national educational reform efforts of the decade, adapting the Outward Bound methodology to the operation of an entire school system. (Over 100 public schools would be using Expeditionary Learning by the end of the decade.) • The Costa Rica Rainforest Outward Bound School opens, with an emphasis on conservation of rainforest as well as adventure activities. • Outward Bound Hong Kong hosts the 1994 international conference.

1995 • Hong Kong Outward Bound opens a branch in China, focused on corporate programmes.

1996 • In the ASEAN Southeast Asian region, Brunei Darussalam begins operations with strong support and leadership from Singapore.

1997 • Finland begins Outward Bound programmes, placing a strong emphasis on training and the accreditation of other adventure programmes in the country. • Bulgaria begins operations on a limited scale. • Thompson Island Outward Bound Education Center is the location of the World Conference in Boston, Massachusetts, USA.

1998 • A unique organisational structure is tested in France using a network of consultants. However, the experiment does not endure and operations would be suspended in 2000. • The World Conference is held at Krochlendorff, hosted by Outward Bound Germany.

1999 • Thailand begins an Outward Bound school with the intention to serve young people and street children.

2000 • Ian Wade takes over as Executive Director of Outward Bound International with a mandate to complete the agreed Safety Reviews. • A new school in Brazil receives a Provisional License. • The World Conference takes place in Sabah, East Malaysia. • The Canadian Outward Bound Wilderness School and Outward Bound Western Canada merge to become one centre, Outward Bound Canada.

2001 • Full licenses are granted to Brunei Darussalam and Sri Lanka and a new school in Korea is launched. • Formalised safety review procedures and leader training begin. • The Netherlands centre and some African countries cease Outward Bound operations. • Outward Bound Switzerland receives exploratory status, with great promise to become a future Outward Bound centre.

2002 • Outward Bound Bali offers its first course. • Regional meetings are well attended in Australia and Europe, and the World Conference is held in Singapore.

Introduction: Ian Wade, Executive Director of Outward Bound International

It is with great pleasure that I introduce to you Outward Bound THE INWARD ODYSSEY volume 2. Since the publication of volume 1 in 1991, much has changed within the Outward Bound International community. The fall of the "iron curtain" and opening up of Eastern Europe has allowed the growth of Outward Bound centres in former "Eastern Block" countries such as Romania, the Czech Republic, Hungary and Slovakia. These centres have brought the innovative education techniques used by Outward Bound to countries searching for new beginnings. In addition, these countries have brought innovation to Outward Bound with programmes that integrate the arts and theatre into personal growth challenges.

There has been extraordinary growth of centres in the ASEAN region led by Singapore, the largest single Outward Bound centre. The vision of that centre has been transformed to serve a nation-building agenda emphasising enterprise, leadership and mutual respect for all races. New centres have been licensed, or significantly expanded, in Brunei, Indonesia and Thailand. Outward Bound has continued its service to other communities, where divisiveness between cultural, racial and ethnic groups occurs. In particular, the fall of Apartheid in South Africa paved the way for Outward Bound to enter this country and work to promote respect and understanding of this nation. Outward Bound has seen growth in Latin America with schools opening in Brazil and Costa Rica.

The last decade has also brought great change for the established centres. The United Kingdom, Germany, Hong Kong, Australia, Canada and the U.S.A. have seen their market leadership position challenged by the numerous competitors inspired by the success of Outward Bound. Each country has responded by making itself more efficient and relevant to the needs of their youth.

Outward Bound has begun to capitalise on its global presence in the last decade by its safety and quality review practices. This "accreditation" process has improved the quality of all centres through risk management review, collaboration on programme development and sharing of staff. The licensing of Outward Bound in new countries is now more structured to ensure that the right factors are present for success, and support is available for new centres to learn from best practises of the past.

Outward Bound International appreciates the dedicated effort of Mark Zelinski in creating for our community a visual depiction of the character of Outward Bound around the world. We hope that through this book you will discover both the strength of our community and the magic of our courses for people of many different cultures and countries. This book shows that the founders' concepts remain timeless in their relevance to the needs and development of people around the world.

Ian Wade
Executive Director

In an intricate maze of tunnels at Outward Bound Belgium, students trek, climb and crawl through dank, narrow passageways and into spectacular chambers, to find their way out of the labyrinth.

EUROPE

ABERDOVEY

Aberdovey is synonymous with Outward Bound. Its co-founders, Kurt Hahn and Laurence Holt, and its first two wardens, Jim Hogan and Freddie Fuller, shaped the place and the movement on a 20-hectare site overlooking the Dovey Estuary in mid-Wales.

Aberdovey was established in 1941 as a Sea School to provide a rigorous, adventurous, pre-sea training course for young men who might go on to help with the Battle of the Atlantic. After meeting its initial goals, the school continued to do a great deal more. From the beginning, community service has been an important part of the programme, especially in the arenas of sea and mountain rescue. Outward Bound staff and students may be called upon to assist in rescues and this is an important part of the training at Outward Bound Wales.

Aberdovey has remained the sailing and water sports centre of the UK Trust, through all of the Trust's change and transitions. The waterfront facility at Outward Bound Wales is fully equipped with a range of kayaks, canoes, dinghies and sailing cutters as well as all the personal equipment, such as wetsuits. The centre has easy access to white water rivers, good surfing and scenic coastal waters. In the evenings, students can practise rolling in a heated pool and learn techniques needed for basic British Canoe Union and Royal Yachting Association qualifications.

For those less interested in technical skills and more interested in personal development, Aberdovey has an array of programmes to meet that need. In their "Aiming Higher" programme, Aberdovey staff have worked with the Birmingham Education Authority to develop an innovative mentoring, adventure and information technology education course. In addition, Aberdovey continues to offer a wide range of programmes for youth, including the classic Outward Bound course.

The waters around Aberdovey offer challenge and diversity, essential elements that made this setting the natural choice for the first Outward Bound centre.

22

Students tackle the daunting challenge of climbing
the weathered cliffs of the Welsh coastline.

The historic town of Aberdovey has been a locale for the trials
and triumphs of the Outward Bound experience since 1941.

23

Early morning glow illuminates the western slopes of Cader Idris as a management group responds to a staged mountain rescue emergency alert.

Outward Bound Eskdale is situated in the picturesque valley of the River Esk, in the remote high fells of England's western Lake District. Its proximity to some of the best rock climbing in the country near Scafell Pike, the highest peak in England, is an added bonus. The centre itself provides everything participants could need. It is set in a splendid 24-hectare garden, complete with a small mountain lake, and includes Lord Rea's Victorian gothic-turreted mansion, called "the Gatehouse," as well as several outbuildings.

Eskdale became The Outward Bound Mountain School in 1950 – the principal mountaineering centre of the United Kingdom. It continues this tradition with professional training for aspiring mountaineers as well as a variety of navigation and rock climbing courses. Eskdale also has a history of providing innovative courses for adults in the UK, and has most recently become the main centre for Outward Bound professional work.

Organisations and adult professionals looking to improve their teamwork skills need look no farther than Outward Bound Eskdale. The team courses are broken down into building, maintaining, rewarding and re-motivating teams. The expert staff at Eskdale also provide programmes for trainees and recent graduates entering the workplace, managers and coordinators of corporate events. They also host the Charity Challenge, which is a three-day corporate team competition designed to raise money for the Outward Bound United Kingdom Trust as well as awareness of Outward Bound programmes.

Canoeists perform trust-building activities at Eskdale's main centre in this picturesque valley of England's Lake District.

Outward Bound courses are usually far removed from urban areas, allowing students the chance to experience wildlife in natural habitats, often for the first time.

Trusting rope and trainer, a woman leans backward over a promontory to abseil a vertical rock face.

Poised for his descent, a young man plunges into the
frigid river below from the bridge at Dalegarth Leap.

photo: Steve Howe

Making use of the natural challenge found on nearby
Wastwater (the deepest lake in England), students
improvise while canoe-rafting.

ULLSWATER

As the operations headquarters for Outward Bound in the United Kingdom (UK), the Ullswater centre has a depth and breadth of offerings that ensure its place in the family of four centres in the UK. Set in a Georgian mansion on the north shore of Ullswater Lake, amidst 7 hectares of woodland at the heart of Wordsworth country, Ullswater participants enjoy Lakeland scrambles, water activities, ropes courses and caving adventures. A high mountain lodge, nestled under Helvellyn, one of the Lake District's highest peaks, is also available to Ullswater students as they go about their adventures.

Courses at Ullswater are well suited for families, school groups, and those seeking technical skills training. The dormitories at Ullswater make it possible for large groups to visit the centre year-round. School and college students comprise 50 percent of Outward Bound UK's course participants. A number of these programmes have been designed to suit educators both in Aberdovey and Ullswater. Courses generally range from three to five days and include induction for new students, geography studies, adventure and challenge, leadership and teamwork. Trainers also visit school sites and deliver short courses.

In addition to programmes for school children, Outward Bound Ullswater offers a number of training courses for college-age students, including technical outdoor recreation skills and "key skills" (required by the government), which include communication, teamwork, problem solving, and improving personal learning skills and performance. Ullswater leads the way in demonstrating a standard of excellence in safety management, as taught in its kayaking, canoeing, mountain leader assessment and skills development courses.

29

Family weekends and day events at Ullswater help expose both parents and youth to the opportunities at Outward Bound, and help improve the quality of communication between parents and children.

Kayak jumping builds confidence in the power of collaboration for a group of engineering apprentices training on the lake at Ullswater.

It's not just another day at the office for a group of managers who race seven and a quarter kilometres over craggy terrain at Gowbarrow Fell.

photo: Steve Howe

By facing demanding physical trials and pulling together in teamwork, students reach towards their potential.

30

"It was like a lifetime of lessons compressed into two weeks. I used every sense, every skill, every limb, every milligram of energy in the shortest space of time possible. I know that this was more than an educational experience because when I try to explain the activities and learning to others, I often can't find the words."

LOCH EIL

Located 193 kilometres north of Glasgow, the Loch Eil centre is a grand highland shooting lodge formerly owned by the Chief of Clan Cameron. Set amongst its own extensive grounds on the foreshore of Loch Eil, it is close to Ben Nevis, Britain's highest mountain, and the venue for many of the centre's climbing activities. Loch Eil's location close to some of Europe's most beautiful and remote true wilderness ideally places it to provide unique walking and canoeing experiences.

Courses at Loch Eil are some of the most adventurous in the United Kingdom. Loch Eil has focused its programmes on the use of the lochs and Scottish coast as well as the rugged mountains and winters of Scotland. Students can choose a multi-day expedition travelling to the centre of the Knoydart wilderness via sea and fresh water lochs, and then climb some of the many summits in the area. They can train on intense winter mountaineering courses and acquire guide certification. They can also choose to experience the classic 17-day Outward Bound course, or they can learn about tide races, passage planning, rescue and the complexities of coastal navigation on a sea kayaking course.

One traditional course that has continued to be successful through the years is the Skye Trek. This 10-day course is designed to help 16- to 18-year olds prepare for taking their own adventures. A typical Skye Trek day starts with packing up tents and carrying equipment to the next campsite, perhaps via remote summits such as Luinne Benn or Sgurr na Ciche. These are demanding mountain days, which require sound wilderness skills. Next, the ferry takes students across to the Isle of Skye to test their skills on an attempt up the famous Inaccessible Pinnacle.

33

The Loch Eil centre has also been involved in developing courses in the Glasgow area to assist and connect with youth from the city. Through the "Raising Achievement" programme, the centre has been able to support the education and growth of more than 5,000 young men and women.

By reaching beyond their perceived limits, students are transformed by awakened self-reliance and perseverance.

A cutter from Outward Bound Loch Eil crosses the Sound of Mull, skimming past the ruins of a 10th-century castle.

*Once crews have mastered the necessary skills,
the expedition is completed without instruction.*

photo: Steve Howe

*Trekking expeditions explore the Scottish Highlands,
one of the few remaining wilderness areas of
Western Europe.*

UK TRUST

The Outward Bound Trust was founded in 1946 in the United Kingdom, inspired by the vision of Kurt Hahn. It enjoys the Patronage of HRH the Duke of Edinburgh. Its mission is "to inspire young people to fulfill their potential through challenging outdoor activities."

Carrying out the Trust's mission, the Outward Bound schools in the United Kingdom have used the mountains and sea as classrooms for over a million young people. The Trust believes that teamwork, endeavour and courage are crucial skills for people to learn in order to make the most of their lives. It also believes strongly that young people should have the opportunity to participate in Outward Bound programmes regardless of their economic circumstances. As a result, the Trust has developed a generous bursary programme that serves about 18,000 young people every year.

The first school was established in Aberdovey, Wales in 1941 as a sailing school. By the 1950s, schools were opened in Scotland, the Lake District and Devon. In the 1960s, Outward Bound associations were founded to develop volunteer enthusiasts who assisted in raising the money that would allow students to attend.

The history of Outward Bound International is interwoven with that of the UK Trust. Representatives from the UK who travelled to foreign countries were often the conduits of the Outward Bound philosophy in its early years. It has been in the UK that many staff from overseas have been trained and inspired to start their own Outward Bound schools. And so the UK has been a centre of the international educational movement of Outward Bound.

By the 1970s, the schools in the UK were suffering from financial difficulties: the Devon school closed and the Moray Sea School moved to Loch Eil. In the 1980s, professional development for managers and supervisors began. This helped to support the financial recovery of the UK schools.

In the 1990s, the UK centres experienced another financial challenge when they began to lose occupancy and pick up debt. In 1995, the management and trustees of The Duke of Edinburgh's Award took over the running of Outward Bound for three years in order to restore financial health and to lay the foundations for future stability. In the late 1990s, by combining overlapping operations, closing centres that were unprofitable and focusing on sales and quality delivery of programmes, the UK schools showed a continually improving operational and financial position, including independence from the Duke of Edinburgh's Award scheme. Their capacity to overcome adversity has been a testament to the character of the schools and the commitment of the staff to Outward Bound. By 2000, Outward Bound UK regained its momentum and re-established itself as the inspirational leader in outdoor education in the United Kingdom.

"I not only acquired leadership skills, I had the time of my life! You have made possible an experience that will follow me and give me strength for a lifetime."

From its early days, Outward Bound Belgium was different than other Outward Bound centres. Founded in 1977 as a joint venture between local universities, physical education institutes and local businesses, Outward Bound Belgium began running short courses in urban and rural environments. Without the luxury of vast amounts of wilderness or a tradition of open-enrollment programmes, the Belgian organisation was forced to find other ways to promote group and individual development.

A strong focus on group and individual dynamics lies at the core of Outward Bound Belgium's educational style. Trainers adapt the programme at each moment to offer the most appropriate learning opportunities for the group and its members. Programmes include a mix of outdoor activities, problem-solving games and team exercises in a five-day or shorter format. Outward Bound Belgium works primarily with existing groups such as schools, universities, companies, social profit teams and socially vulnerable youth.

Since 1980, the school's base has been a country house located in the Belgian Ardennes. This old mansion has room for two groups to sleep, meet, cook and eat, and is set amongst a landscape of forests and fields near the River Meuse and its tributaries. This limestone region offers a variety of possibilities for outdoor challenges. Participants take part in rock climbing, abseiling, caving, "via ferrata" (a climbing activity in the mountains that makes use of fixed belay cables), ropes courses, hiking, camping, river crossings and dynamics (problem-solving activities).

Although Outward Bound Belgium has traditionally worked primarily in Flemish, the organisation continues to diversify its offerings by expanding its French and English language programmes. It also offers experiential education "train-the-trainer" programmes for teachers and youth workers, and long-term programmes, particularly for socially vulnerable youth.

The Belgian Ardennes is dotted with countless limestone caves. Moving through dark caverns of cold rock, students must squeeze down a chute called the "birthing canal" to find their route back to the surface far above.

Without verbal communication, a team needs ingenuity and original thinking to advance "the caterpillar".

Given limited time and materials with which to construct a raft, corporate participants race against the clock to paddle across the River Meuse and back.

In this pastoral region of forests, rivers and rocky hillsides, a human chain ascends "de schuine helling" (the steep slope).

41

42

Participants meet physical challenges in urban settings, perform community service and work with disadvantaged citizens and the elderly, developing compassion and sensitivity in the city core.

photo: Luk Peeters

Courses in the Spanish Pyrenees bring a fresh ambience to the Outward Bound experience.

Positioned on a rocky pinnacle, a young woman extends herself across an abyss to ascend a sheer cliff, realising a far greater potential than she had ever previously dared to explore.

Emotional reactions to an activity can vary dramatically. Caring and compassion from within the group brings comfort in a moment of stress.

GERMANY

A capsule history of Outward Bound Germany reveals that the country's first mountain school at Baad first welcomed students in 1956. Four more centres have been established since then, including one in Eastern Germany, created after the fall of the Berlin Wall. Each centre has its own flavour and type of courses, inspired by its particular environment.

At Baad, students can enjoy year-round courses that include skiing, mountaineering, hiking, rafting and climbing. The centre is encircled by the Austrian Alps – a perfect setting for outdoor adventures. Close by is Outward Bound Germany's busiest centre, Schwangau. Founded in 1996, it rests by a picturesque lake nestled in the foothills of the magnificent Alps.

Far to the north, on the opposite side of the country, is Königsburg. Situated on the banks of the Schlei Fjord, Königsburg is the centre of Outward Bound Germany's summer sailing courses. Here, at the sea school, programmes focus on ecological projects like water investigation, understanding environmental problems, wildlife conservation and nature management.

A third centre, Schloss Krochlendorff, a splendid old building surrounded by parks, offers a ropes course, canoeing, expeditioning, hiking and biking. At this centre, Outward Bound Germany offers management-training programmes for corporations from around the country.

45

At Schweriner See, the only centre in Eastern Germany, students have the opportunity to kayak on a lake and travel to an island for additional activities.

Outward Bound Germany has also become involved in developing mobile courses to take to school campuses and corporations. Most of its current business is with schools and apprentices on one- to two-week adventures. It also offers "train-the-trainer" courses for professionals, courses for non-profit youth organisations, and one-day "exposure courses". Guests are accommodated on site.

Youngsters follow their instructor to a hilltop at sunset during the odyssey of self-discovery and personal growth that is at the heart of the Outward Bound adventure.

46

Corporate trainees raise multi-coloured sails against
a grey sea during their Baltic expedition.

An instructor intentionally capsises an occupied kayak as
an introduction to flat-water paddling at OB Schweriner See.

An expedition on wheels, students cycle through rural villages and rolling hills of the German countryside.

During white water rafting, crew members alternate as captain, making split-second decisions and reading the river as it unfolds before them.

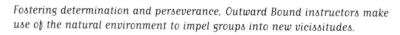
Fostering determination and perseverance, Outward Bound instructors make use of the natural environment to impel groups into new vicissitudes.

As the final obstacle of a demanding mountaineering expedition, groups cross a deep river gorge at Outward Bound Baad.

Outward Bound **Germany**

"I fully experienced the power of team spirit. I treasured the trust and care among team members, and realised the critical elements and techniques to achieve an effective team. This was the most memorable, rewarding and challenging experience in my life."

CZECH REPUBLIC

"All the problems and conflicts of the world are reflected in each of us and the world is a reflection of ourselves. Therefore, we can seek the key to their solution from within."

This is the motto of Vacation School Lipnice, the non-profit division of Outward Bound Czech Republic.

This school has been in existence since 1977. It became a member of Outward Bound in the early 1990s, when staff realised that its work and philosophy were similar to Outward Bound schools around the world. The philosophy of the Vacation School Lipnice has its roots in the ancient Greek word kalokagathia, which symbolises the concept of ideal nurturing through the harmonious development of outward merits, inner beauty and moral principles. The performance of physically, mentally and socially challenging activities within natural environments helps students reach kalokagathia.

Outward Bound Czech Republic also has a for-profit arm that serves professionals in outdoor training programmes. This centre was the first of its kind in the Czech Republic. Profits from this organisation support the programmes of the Vacation School.

Since its inclusion in the Outward Bound International community, Outward Bound Czech Republic has encouraged new programme elements such as art, theatre and creative expression as a part of Outward Bound courses. A process called "dramaturgy" links and intertwines course experiences for the participants. The staff at Outward Bound Czech Republic see themselves as artists rather than technicians, creating and developing a course that changes with the needs of the students. The result: memorable experiences and intense human relations that help students find within themselves unexpected sources of energy, self-confidence and spontaneous creativity.

Communication of feelings and ideas is paramount to courses in the Czech Republic, where group discussions are sometimes held in an atmosphere of historical significance.

photo: Pepa Streda

Using various means of creative expression, instructors guide their groups through imaginative and often therapeutic activities such as body-painting.

Working artistically as a team, students are in a unique position to learn about themselves and their companions through painting, theatre and even the creation of Tibetan sand-paintings.

Reassured by her instructor, a participant meets the trial of abseiling, one of the more traditional Outward Bound activities offered at OB Czech Republic.

53

On the last night of the course, a feast is followed by a festive bonfire party, and the group has a last chance to share its Outward Bound experience together.

Having achieved so much together physically and emotionally, the greatest challenge can sometimes be to say goodbye upon course completion.

SLOVAKIA

Dressed in the costumes of a king and a queen, the instructors of Outward Bound Slovakia – also known as the Studio of Experience – lead their students on both a physical and a creative journey into their own personal and professional development. In addition to classic physical activities, the instructors at this Outward Bound school work hard to create an artistic studio environment in which participants can refashion their self-images. This is part of the unique contribution Outward Bound Slovakia has made to the international community of Outward Bound schools.

A student on a course in Slovakia may find himself or herself building an ice cave during the day and then donning a costume and acting at night. Students can climb, abseil, cave, raft and participate in ropes challenges. Alongside this, they can express themselves creatively through theatre, film and artistic workshops. Some of Outward Bound Slovakia's participants have found the creative aspects of the programme more demanding than the physical challenges.

The idea of the Studio of Experience came after the break-up of Czechoslovakia. Tamara Greksakova and friends, who had been connected with the Czech school, wanted to offer Outward Bound in the mountains and cities of the new Slovak Republic. After travelling around the world and looking at Outward Bound models, Outward Bound Slovakia chose to create shorter programmes of one to 12 days in duration.

Courses fall into three distinct categories: open enrollment for youth, university students, parents and children, youth at risk, orphans and youth workers; professional development programmes for industry and corporations in Slovakia and Eastern Europe; and international courses with students from as close as Croatia and as far away as Singapore.

Courses vary in location depending on their type. Creative-expressive and city-challenge courses are run from Bratislava, the capital of Slovakia. Outdoor courses are located in the central mountains of the country, including the High and Low Tatras, Big Fatra, and the Small Carpathian Mountains.

"I will take home a new sense of confidence, responsibility, physical ability, and independence. I will take home a culture that I cannot wait to share with others I know. I have learned so many lessons about working with others and communicating."

Outward Bound Romania is all about creating and building community. Since its founding in 1993 by Imre Fodor, a civic leader in the city of Tirgu-Mures, it has developed and implemented programmes for more than 5,000 young people and community leaders.

These programmes not only instill local people with self-confidence through standard Outward Bound activities, but also work towards building better communities by offering skills such as conflict resolution, project development, fundraising and organisational development. In one rural development project, students have gone on to create local community service organisations that have continued to thrive and serve the people of Romania.

Other courses focus on creating harmony between the multiplicity of ethnic groups and cultures in the region. In March 1990, fighting broke out in Tirgu-Mures between parts of the Hungarian and Romanian populations. In May 2000, Outward Bound organised a programme with 24 participants — bringing together 12 Romanians and 12 Hungarians from this region. Through this type of programme, Outward Bound teaches diplomacy, youth leadership and tolerance.

As Outward Bound Romania expands, it continues to serve economically disadvantaged youth, orphans, social workers and educators in the region. It also serves professionals and international clients through cross-cultural courses.

Surrounded by the Carpathian Mountains, Outward Bound Romania enjoys an ideal location for trekking, abseiling, climbing, community projects (ecological, intercultural), expeditions (bike, kayak or cross-country skiing) and orienteering. As well as giving students from Romania and abroad a great intercultural experience, Outward Bound Romania also offers activities that teach participants about the arts and crafts of the region.

At Outward Bound Romania's main base camp, participants tackle "the Wall". The challenge is to scale the four-and-a-half-metre-high smooth surface without the aid of ropes or equipment.

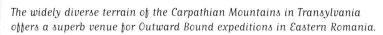
The widely diverse terrain of the Carpathian Mountains in Transylvania offers a superb venue for Outward Bound expeditions in Eastern Romania.

On the final leg of a three-week international expedition, participants trade their kayaks for bicycles, and rivers are replaced by the city streets of Tirgu-Mures, home of Outward Bound Romania's headquarters.

Outward Bound **Romania**

In Transylvanian canyons, the wilderness itself becomes a classroom.

HUNGARY

Outward Bound Hungary

In 1990, a team of Hungarians, sponsored by Rainer Güttler (the managing director of Outward Bound Germany at the time), gathered together with the aim of founding Outward Bound Hungary. Over a period of two years, two separate teams of staff took instructor courses at the Colorado Outward Bound School as preparation for starting their own school. This was a tremendous opportunity given the dramatic changes occurring in Eastern Europe at the time.

By 1995, these two separate groups simultaneously decided to get Outward Bound afloat in Hungary. The two organisations offered similar programmes but acted independently from one another. Through mutual connection to Outward Bound Romania, the two groups in Hungary began to learn more about one another. Although it took some time for the organisations to recognise it, their missions complemented each other splendidly. One organisation was founded by the Hungarian Nature-Lover Association and emphasised the training of children and adults. The other, founded by KVIF (College for Trade, Catering and Tourist Industry), specialised in programmes for university students. On October 20th, 2000, the holiday celebrating the creation of the Republic of Hungary, the two groups decided to unite and become Outward Bound Hungary.

It is a part of the Hungarian school's legend that its founding capital was two dollars. Now they have an office, storage facility and base camp situated in the Danube-Ipoly National Park among the Börzsöny Mountains. The backbone of the organisation is 20 enthusiastic instructors. Adapting to the natural conditions in Hungary, they offer courses that include rock climbing, caving, canoeing, raft-building and a portable ropes course to take to different sites. They now offer courses for 1,200 participants annually on two- to three-day long programmes for university students, corporate groups and children.

"During the training I was very much confronted with the impact of my behaviour and my way of working with others. For me this was the most important aspect of the training and it changed my way of working."

FINLAND

The idea for an Outward Bound school in Finland arose in 1993 after a Finnish group of representatives from different fields of Finnish youth work visited Outward Bound Königsburg in Germany. Soon after, members of this team pushed to open an Outward Bound school in the small town of Nurmes in North Karelia near the eastern border. By 1994, Finland received its licensing from Outward Bound International and began operations with Finnish youth in North Karelia, South Karelia, Southern Finland and Lapland (above the Arctic circle).

Courses range from two- to 14-days duration – the most popular being a five-day experiential education course. Outward Bound Finland is positioning itself as the expert in experiential training and outdoor safety in Finland. To accomplish this, it offers a number of leadership courses for wilderness guides as well as safety training programmes. In addition, Outward Bound Finland's courses include youth at risk programmes, college courses, youth and social worker training and corporate courses.

Adventure elements available to participants in Finland include trekking, canoeing, cross-country skiing, and church boat rowing. Rowing the church boat is a traditional way of travelling in Finland – each small village once possessed a rowboat for 10 to 16 persons that would be used to get to church on Sundays. Today, rowing a church boat has been adopted as an excellent group task to build teamwork and coordination.

In the tradition of the Vikings, students row in rhythm across the lakes of Eastern Finland in "church boats", used for centuries by rural folk for their Sunday migration to worship.

Problem-solving activities help participants in planning, setting goals and objectives, time-management and communication.

Nights spent near base-camp are accompanied by a cherished Finnish custom – sauna – which is usually followed by a cold swim in the lake.

From the vantage point of her makeshift shelter, a student watches the moon rise
over Eastern Karelia in anticipation of the first night of her solo adventure.

Mornings at Outward Bound Kenya begin early. As it descends the slope of Mount Kilimanjaro, an expedition watches the retreat of dawn's mist reveal a magnificent view of the Kuku Plain ahead.

KENYA

Outward Bound Kenya

Outward Bound Trust of Kenya is the third oldest Outward Bound school in the world, the first and second being those at Aberdovey in Wales and Eskdale in England. Based in Loitokitok, on the slopes of the majestic Kilimanjaro, the highest mountain in Africa, the school was opened in 1951 by Sir Everling Barling, the former Governor of Kenya. The first warden was D.A. Lake, a former college principal, who took on the challenge to spearhead the institution.

Outward Bound Trust of Kenya was later expanded to embrace Tanzania and Uganda (which were formerly British Colonies), thus becoming Outward Bound East Africa. The staff were drawn from the three countries up until 1976, when the community of East Africa dissolved.

In the 1980s, the school experienced extreme financial difficulties, but managed to get back on track in 1989 with a financial boost from USAID. Gaining its "second wind", Outward Bound Kenya has since experienced immense growth. This has been possible under the visionary leadership of Marsden Madoka (retired Major), Executive Chairman and Major James Oswago, Executive Director.

Outward Bound Trust of Kenya has a three-pronged approach to its experiential training: Pre-Course Survey; Actual Training; and Post-Course Impact Assessment Survey. The growth of its client base attests to the success of this programme.

A very busy school with a wide range of activities, it serves children; youth; corporate clients; special groups, including street children, youth at risk and those traumatized and dismembered by disasters; organised groups from other Outward Bound schools and international centres; and community-based programmes such as micro-finance institutions, church-based organisations and local NGOs.

Apart from its main base of operations on the slopes of Mount Kilimanjaro, the school has a head office located in Kenya's capital and commercial city, Nairobi, where the administrative and marketing offices are housed. The school also has base camps especially suited to its mobile courses, which are carried out in the Maasai plains, Mount Kenya and Mount Kilimanjaro campsites and Rhino Rock Climbing Site.

Extending its course locations, Outward Bound Trust of Kenya also uses hired facilities: Kanamai – Mombasa at Kenya's coastal line, Kenya Wildlife Service Institute – Naivasha in the basin of Kenya's great Rift Valley, and Naromoru River Lodge at the gateway to Mount Kilimanjaro.

Major James Oswago captures the essence of this school when he says, "At the roof of Africa, you get a unique experience. The serenity is music to the ear. The breeze provided by the indigenous African forest makes you younger, it eliminates stress and heralds a new beginning."

In training for a final expedition to Mount Kenya, a student scales the sheer face of Rhino Rock.

Zebra, giraffe and elephants roam in abundance on the Kuku Plain. These lands are protected by the Maasai tribe, who regard the animals as their friends.

Without the use of their hands, the task of passing a tennis ball to teammates becomes an exercise in interaction and intimacy.

Having tested themselves to new limits, students of all ages return home with greater insight and confidence.

The base camp of Outward Bound Kenya is located on the slopes of Africa's highest peak. Mount Kilimanjaro.

Students may hike 20 kilometres of astonishing terrain in a day. but the real adventure takes place within their hearts and minds.

Outward Bound **Kenya**

Located at the base of the Chimanimani Mountains within the Chimanimani National Park on the eastern border of Zimbabwe, this Outward Bound school has worked hard to serve as a conduit for positive change in a country wrought with political and economic turmoil.

The school's history consists of two distinct phases. The original school was founded in 1961 and from the beginning worked to support multi-racial and multi-ethnic courses in the region. Unfortunately, the thriving school was forced to close in 1976 due to the dangers of guerilla warfare in Eastern Rhodesia. Eleven years later, with the help of staff from the United Kingdom, the centre reopened as Outward Bound Zimbabwe. Although political turmoil has not subsided, the school continues to operate, maintaining its commitment to working with a broad spectrum of Zimbabweans, from school children to corporate managers. Thanks to a strong funding base, the school is financially stable, despite the severe economic crisis within the country.

Quality of courses has not been sacrificed in spite of all the challenges. Students on an Outward Bound Zimbabwe course can spend three to 20 days exploring the true wilds of Eastern Zimbabwe, where they can see elephants, lions, buffalos, black rhinos and leopards as well as enjoy high mountain views and spectacular waterfalls. One unique activity has been dubbed the "Temple of Doom", a long traverse through a huge cleft in a rock face. The name comes from a couple of house-sized boulders wedged above the students' heads as they walk through.

Outward Bound Zimbabwe has also become the leading expert in outdoor education in this region and it now offers wilderness search and rescue courses. These have been adapted for training mine rescue teams from across Zimbabwe. In addition, the centre is looking to develop outdoor professionals by offering a mountaincraft and leadership course.

Youngsters pool their resources to assemble a raft in an environment where prejudice and preconceived social norms are abandoned.

74

The Haroni River transforms into a magnificent waterfall cascading into Tessa's Pool. Here, a team forms a human pyramid in order to ring a bell from an improvised raft.

Physical activities are used to help develop a positive attitude and the skill to adapt to an ever-changing environment.

Through rock climbing, participants are encouraged to face risk not as a threat but as an opportunity.

SOUTH AFRICA

To Serve, To Strive
And Not To Yield

In the early 1990s, Charles P. Stetson had a vision of bringing Outward Bound to South Africa to help heal the racial divides. By 1991, with the fall of apartheid, he had found the right team to found Outward Bound South Africa and the school opened its doors. By the mid 1990s, the school was operating courses for youth at risk, the street youth of South Africa, schools and corporations.

In addition to the international mission of Outward Bound, Outward Bound South Africa has its own intensely-felt mission: "To promote greater understanding between people, especially the young, of different races and cultures. To work together to remove the barriers which separate the people of the world." As a result, the school focuses on courses that intervene in the lives of young people who are trapped in cycles of poverty, crime, violence and unemployment. It helps people discover that a disadvantaged past does not have to mean a disadvantaged future, or as Hahn would put it: "Your disability is your opportunity."

To reach a diverse crowd, Outward Bound South Africa offers a wide variety of courses. These range from three to 21 days in duration and include hiking, camping, orienteering, abseiling, rock climbing, sailing, canoeing, kayaking and rafting. Locations include Willow Point, the school's base camp next to the Swartvlei at the foot of the Outeniqua Mountain range, mobile operations in the Sterkfontein Nature Reserve, where bouldering and rock climbing are the main course activities, and the breathtaking Valley of a Thousand Hills, where groups can embark upon particularly challenging expeditions.

77

It takes compassion and commitment to be an Outward Bound instructor. An instructor must be an excellent facilitator with an acute interest in the growth and development of others.

The courses, which often begin with a morning run, offer participants the chance to discover a new sense of self-worth and achievement, compassion and service to others.

Guiding a teammate through the centre of the "Spider Web" without touching the ropes is difficult.

78

Students struggle to sustain the cadence required to hold true the vessel's course on the vlei near Willow Point base.

*Millions have experienced the trials and triumphs of an Outward Bound
adventure. For many, their lives have been profoundly changed.*

"I've realised how beautiful is the world and the importance of the environment during this course. Now I have a brave heart and a bold memory."

An Outward Bound Canada marathon begins in the glistening dawn of Ontario's Black Sturgeon Lake.
Setting new limits for themselves and often surpassing them, students re-define what is possible.

CANADA

Looking for beautiful, rugged country and the companionship of fellow adventurers? Look no further than Outward Bound Canada. Outward Bound Canada has three operations in Ontario, two in British Columbia, and mobile programmes in the Yukon Territory and Alberta.

The wilderness is Outward Bound Canada's classroom. The lakes, rivers, forests, mountains and ocean provide the challenges. Some of these challenges are physical, as when paddling a sea kayak into the rolling waves, climbing a rugged peak, sailing on the ocean, leading a team of sled dogs, or portaging a canoe through a boreal forest. Other challenges include developing leadership skills or learning to work effectively as a member of a team.

At Chetwynd, the national headquarters of Outward Bound Canada, staff work year-round with schools and corporations, offering courses from seven to 14 days long. Chetwynd also accommodates a semester high school programme for students interested in expeditionary learning. Nestled on Black Sturgeon Lake, in the thickly wooded forest of spruce and balsam fir (160 kilometres north of Thunder Bay), is Homeplace, where students embark on 21-day or longer canoeing courses in the summer, and dog sledding and ski courses in the winter. Closer to the shores of Lake Superior lies a mobile site on White River, where students participate in canoeing and hiking courses.

85

Deep in the rugged, glaciated coastal range of British Columbia, on the western side of the country, is the Bennett Mountaineering Base. Groups can travel for weeks in unspoiled wilderness among these mountains. It is here that Canada's mountaineering (on foot or on skis) and rugged backpacking courses take place. British Columbia is also home to sailing and sea kayaking courses in and around the wild and beautiful Pacific coastal waters between British Columbia's mainland and Northern Vancouver Island.

Outward Bound Canada strives to provide "adventures that last a lifetime" for both youth and adults of all ages. Community programmes include leadership development training for aboriginal people, "Women of Courage" courses (for survivors of domestic violence) and youth at risk courses. There is a generous bursary programme for students burdened by economic hardship.

Much different than the inexperienced crew who ventured into the North Gulf Islands of British Columbia three weeks earlier, these seasoned sailors push homeward with new skills, new strengths and new-found friends.

86

It is unlikely that students will encounter other human beings during their mobile course in the extraordinary alpine wilderness of Western Canada's Coast Mountains.

As an added bonus to the thrill of rappelling the 50-metre surface of Claghorn, students can enjoy a majestic view of Northern Ontario's boreal forest.

The consequence of facing challenge can sometimes be a startling new awareness, as a kayak novice discovers on a frothing section of the Gull River.

As navigation and other essential wilderness skills are mastered, students take turns leading their Lake Superior expedition.

Shouldering heavy backpacks across the rugged, dramatic terrain of Lake Superior's shoreline, students develop strength, stamina and a deep connection to each other.

89

The tranquillity of a Georgian Bay sunset creates memories that will last a lifetime.

PACIFIC CREST

The Pacific Crest Outward Bound School (PCOBS) has its roots in the Northwestern United States. It was founded in 1965 as the Northwest Outward Bound School. As time went on, its leaders recognised the outstanding educational value of the wilderness of the Pacific Crest and Sierra Mountains and by 1983, the school had operations in California, Idaho, Washington, Oregon and Baja, Mexico. To reflect its expanded character, the Northwest School changed its name to the Pacific Crest School.

Since its founding, PCOBS has emphasised the mobile wilderness course. Students arrive straight from the airport to the course base, which might be a granite mountain or the mouth of a river or the entrance to a forest. There they learn how to carefully pack their backpacks, float safely down river or navigate through desert scrub. At Pacific Crest Outward Bound, wilderness is both the context and catalyst for personal growth for youth and adults, including members of professional organisations. To promote diversity and personal development for all students, the school supports a strong scholarship programme for urban youth from the cities of the Western United States. Most courses are between five and 25 days long, but the school also offers 78-day semester courses.

The characteristics of the natural terrain are challenging enough to teach many useful lessons. Nevertheless, the instructors at PCOBS are constantly looking for new ways to bring out leadership and teamwork in their students. This might take the form of a group learning how to rescue themselves in the midst of white water rapids or belaying each other to the top of an 3,300-metre-high peak.

The philosophy and practices of the Pacific Crest School are nicely expressed by the words of Willi Unsoeld, one of the early leaders of the school: "Why not stay out there in the wilderness the rest of your days? Because that's not where men and women are. The final test for me of the legitimacy of the experience is how well your experience of the sacred in nature enables you to cope more effectively with the problems of humankind when you come back to the city."

In the high desert of California's Joshua Tree National Monument, students develop a better understanding of themselves and a deeper respect for their natural surroundings.

92

Teams carefully traverse a lava field in central Oregon. Environmental preservation is a central component of courses at the Pacific Crest Outward Bound School.

Sailing students acquire a greater awareness about themselves and their fellow crew members and develop respect, affection and trust for one another.

Communication and teamwork are vital to summit in the southern Sierra Mountains.

The Colorado Outward Bound School (COBS) was founded on the slopes of the Rocky Mountains above the small community of Marble, Colorado, in 1961. The following year, the school featured the first Outward Bound course for youth in America. As with the original Outward Bound School in Aberdovey, Wales, COBS was founded as a result of a collaborative effort between educators and industrialists. Businessmen in Colorado, concerned about youth who seemed unwilling to accept responsibility and challenge, wanted a "school" that would provide character-building experiences to young people. They worked with educators Charles Froelicher, John Holden, Jack Snobble, Joshua Miner and Captain Fuller from the Aberdovey School to help establish the first Outward Bound school in the United States.

More than forty years later, the Colorado Outward Bound School continues to instill a sense of leadership, service and self-discovery in each of its students. Courses are offered in Colorado, Utah, Wyoming, Alaska, Arizona, California and Baja, Mexico, and range in length from five to 81 days.

The school prides itself on offering courses for people from all walks of life, from age 14 and older. COBS has continuously expanded its offerings and now includes courses for adults, business professionals and community groups. Course activities include mountaineering, white water rafting, rock climbing, sea kayaking, backpacking, canyoneering and backcountry snowboarding.

95

The Colorado Outward Bound School continues to embody and endorse the principles first articulated by Kurt Hahn — to train those "who would not shirk from leadership and who would, when called upon, make independent decisions, put right action before expediency, and the common cause before personal ambition, bettering the world, one person at a time."

During a placid interval between rapids, rafting teams are able to appreciate the grandeur of Utah's Lodore Canyon.

photo: Jimbo Buickerood

On course in Baja, Mexico, a sea-kayaking experience is combined with an additional inter-cultural element

photo: Brian Litz

The physical demands of the Outward Bound experience summon new resources from within — this is also a deeply inward journey.

Rock climbing, one of the few activities that students face alone, is an experience that tests them physically, emotionally and spiritually.

The reward of witnessing animals in the wild can help students to appreciate the interdependency of all life.

97

Having studied the rapids from shore, students need the synergy of teamwork to successfully negotiate the forceful currents of the Green River.

"Rivers are a very powerful learning tool. Students learn how to work with the river; overpowering it is futile, but sound decision-making is imperative. Running rivers is like running life."

VOYAGEUR

The wilds of the Boundary Waters in Minnesota and Canada were the setting for the first courses offered by Minnesota Outward Bound School in 1964. Like the trappers and traders before them, students at Voyageur Outward Bound School (the name was changed in 1983) go on expeditions in their canoes and on dog sleds through the 400,000 hectares and thousands of lakes in this pine-forested region at the centre of the North American continent. It is still one of the only places left in the lower 48 states where people can travel for days or weeks without seeing a house or road.

From its canoeing and voyageur roots, this Outward Bound school expanded to include courses on the Rio Grande in Texas, the Northern Rocky Mountains of Montana, the Great Lakes, and the urban areas of the Midwestern United States. Today, the school offers climbing, white water canoeing, expedition canoeing, backpacking, dog sledding, inland sea kayaking and cross-cultural courses. They have blended the classic with the innovative, offering traditional 14- and 22-day courses as well as courses designed for women, educators, couples, families, youth at risk, and those in search of life and career renewal.

Voyageur's philosophy of education is to help people discover and develop their character by focusing on personal and psychological peaks rather than geologic ones. As a result, compassion becomes a key theme on courses. "A large measure of the fulfillment in life stems from compassion for self and others, expressed through caring and being cared for." (Voyageur Instructor Handbook)

A spectacular arena for addressing fear and taking action, the ropes course at Voyageur's main Minnesota base features a network of events ranging from low heights to heights of more than 20 metres.

Hauling komatiks laden with supplies, dog-team expeditions traverse Northern Minnesota's winter wilderness of frozen lakes, rivers and forests.

A strenuous journey through Montana's Beartooth Range is rewarded with exquisite alpine vistas.

103

Canoeists ride the Rio Grande River, flanked on one side of the river by the Chihuahuan Desert of Mexico and by Texas on the other.

NORTH CAROLINA

photo: NCOBS

North Carolina Outward Bound School's first crew in 1967, known as "NC 1," was a group of teenage boys backpacking in the Linville Gorge Wilderness of North Carolina. Today's students are male and female, teenagers and adults. In addition to the Appalachian Mountains, the course areas have grown to include the North Carolina Outer Banks, Florida's Ten Thousand Islands, the Bahamas and the Chilean Andes. In 1967, the school had fewer than 50 alumni. By 2002, the 35th anniversary, it had more than 60,000.

North Carolina's base camps are located near some of the most diverse and exciting multi-pitch rock climbing sites and white water paddling rivers in the United States. The expanded programme includes mountain biking on more than 300 kilometres of mountain-bike trails in the Pisgah National Forest. In Florida and the Bahamas, students can sea kayak through hundreds of undeveloped islands while listening to island birds chattering from nesting refuges along the shore. Some of the courses take students snorkeling through exotic coral reefs for close-up views of butterfly fish, moray eels and dolphins. Further south, North Carolina Outward Bound has opened up courses in the glaciated and densely forested Chilean Andes, where the school offers mountaineering courses and international leadership semester courses.

Regardless of the territory or course type, North Carolina Outward Bound's core values and curriculum have stood the test of time. Since the time of the very first crew, the school's staff have remained true to their goal – to provide students with challenging adventures that emphasise self-reliance, fitness, craftsmanship, compassion and leadership in a wilderness setting.

Participants arrive with their own goals – shaped by the daily trials of a private life – but quickly find themselves drawn into an experience that challenges them physically and psychologically.

Near Green Cove base, an instructor gives words of
advice and encouragement to a 65-year-old climber.

The wild and scenic Chattooga River carries canoe
expeditions into the heartland of the South.

Students now have the opportunity to embark upon mountain
biking expeditions in the Pisgah National Forest.

Plunging into the waterfall, groups are
quickly immersed in one of the Chattooga's
ever-changing conditions, which range
from gentle flow to cascading torrent.

NEW YORK CITY

"Youth today are misled by a society which dictates how they should behave rather than simply being themselves. By providing youth with the opportunity to discover who they are and the power they hold, we can help them become the answer to today's problems. It is time to give our youth the chance to stand out and allow them to lead us." (A founding member of Rebels with a Cause, a New York City Outward Bound Center alumni programme)

In 1987, sufficient energy and enthusiasm abounded in New York City to inspire the creation of a one-of-a-kind centre to effect positive and lasting change in the lives of the city's young people. For example, programmes were put in place to enable academically challenged youth to learn how to enjoy reading and writing. A good indicator of its overall quality programming is that the students keep coming back for more. This is one of the strengths of the unique urban programmes offered by the New York City Outward Bound Center (NYCOBC).

Today, NYCOBC continues to fulfill its mission through comprehensive school reform, targeted school programmes, professional development programmes for educators, organisational development programmes for schools and non-profit organisations, adventure programmes for youth and after-school and summer programmes. Activities are run year-round and include ropes courses, sailing, canoeing, hiking (urban and wilderness), academic studies, service projects, rock climbing and cultural immersions.

It is clear that students who have attended NYCOBC have had life-changing experiences. Perhaps the words of one literacy and environmental leadership student sum up the effect most eloquently: "Many lessons are taught, but it's up to you to use the knowledge from those lessons. If knowledge is power, then Outward Bound makes you invincible. If the pen is mightier than the sword, then Outward Bound has an unstoppable army. If your strength comes from your soul, then Outward Bound can make you lift a mountain. When you leave this programme, your eyes get wider."

Outward Bound programmes were once conducted exclusively in the wilderness. New York City's Outward Bound Center transfers the same principles of leadership and self-reliance to an urban setting.

110

Outward Bound students at South Bronx High School pose in front of a mural they created as a tribute to a slain classmate.

On NYCOBC's alpine tower in Brooklyn, it quickly becomes clear that the limits to a student's own potential are mostly imagined and self-imposed.

Working together towards a common goal, corporate participants help each other through the "spider web" in Central Park.

"This was the hardest thing I have ever done in my life, but it is also the best thing."

EXPEDITIONARY LEARNING

photo: Maer Rubley

In the late 1980s and early 1990s, a new movement in Outward Bound began in the United States, called Expeditionary Learning. A group of dynamic educators centered at Harvard University and New York City Outward Bound Center began to develop the concept of large-scale school reform based on the tenets of Kurt Hahn and Outward Bound.

The Idea: Emphasise learning by doing, with a particular focus on character growth, teamwork, reflection and literacy. At the same time, assist teachers in connecting high-quality academic learning to adventure, service and character development through a variety of interdisciplinary, project-based learning expeditions.

The Principles: Expeditionary Learning must be connected to the roots of Outward Bound, the Seven Laws of Salem, and the contemporary work of Eleanor Duckworth and Paul Ylvisaker from Harvard University Graduate School of Education. The result: The 10 design principles that every Expeditionary Learning Outward Bound school follows:

1. THE PRIMACY OF SELF-DISCOVERY

Learning happens best with emotion, challenge and the requisite support. People discover their abilities, values, grand passions and responsibilities in situations that offer adventure and the unexpected. They must have tasks that require perseverance, fitness, craftsmanship, imagination, self-discipline and significant achievement. A primary job of the educator is to help students to overcome their fears and to discover their innate capacities and potential.

2. THE HAVING OF WONDERFUL IDEAS

Encourage children's curiosity about the world by creating learning situations that provide material to ponder, time to experiment and time to make sense of what is observed. Foster a community where students' and adults' ideas are respected.

3. RESPONSIBILITY FOR LEARNING

Learning is both a personal process of discovery and a social activity. Each of us learns within and for ourselves and as a part of a group. Every aspect of a school must encourage children, young people and adults to become increasingly responsible for directing their own personal and collective learning.

As their class project, senior high-school students build a house for an underprivileged family, in cooperation with the Housing Authority in Ronan, Montana.

4. INTIMACY AND CARING

Learning is fostered best in small groups where there is trust, sustained caring and mutual respect among all members of the learning community. Keep schools and learning groups small. Be sure there is a caring adult looking after the progress of each child. Arrange for the older students to mentor the younger ones.

5. SUCCESS AND FAILURE

All students must be assured a fair measure of success in learning in order to nurture the confidence and capacity to take risks and rise to increasingly difficult challenges. But it is also important to experience failure, to overcome negative inclinations, to prevail against adversity and to learn how to turn disadvantages into opportunities.

6. COLLABORATION AND COMPETITION

Integrate individual and group development so that the values of friendship, trust and camaraderie are made manifest. Encourage students to compete not against each other, but against their own personal expectations. Instill within students rigorous standards of excellence.

7. DIVERSITY AND INCLUSIVITY

Diversity and inclusivity in all groups dramatically increase richness of ideas, creative power, problem-solving ability and acceptance of others. Encourage students to investigate, value and draw upon their own personal histories, talents and resources together with those of other communities and cultures. Keep the schools and learning groups heterogeneous.

8. THE NATURAL WORLD

A direct and respectful relationship with the natural world refreshes the human spirit and reveals the important lessons of recurring cycles and cause and effect. Students learn to become stewards of the earth and guardians of the generations to come.

9. SOLITUDE AND REFLECTION

Solitude, reflection and silence replenish our energies and open our minds. Be sure students have time alone to explore their own thoughts, make their own connections and create their own ideas. Then give them opportunities to exchange their reflections with each other and with adults.

10. SERVICE AND COMPASSION

We are crew, not passengers, and are strengthened by acts of consequential service to others. One of a school's primary functions is to prepare its students with the attitudes and skills to learn from and be of service to others. At the heart of Expeditionary Learning are five core practices:

Learning Expeditions — Learning expeditions are long-term, multidisciplinary explorations of a single theme, such as the geology of caves, the civil rights movement, water quality, or Galileo's theories. Harnessing the power of adventure and discovery, expeditions take students on intellectual journeys with challenging projects, fieldwork and opportunities to serve, culminating in peak performances.

Reflection and Critique — At Expeditionary Learning schools, teachers exemplify and elicit a culture of reflection, critique, revision and collaboration. Students practise and hone their skills and attitudes until they and their teachers are fully satisfied with the end product.

School Culture — Expeditionary Learning schools promote a strong culture of best effort, high expectations, collaboration, service and diversity. School structures and policies support an environment where adults and young people feel emotionally and physically safe, and feel free to take risks and exceed their perceived limits.

School Structure — Expeditionary Learning requires the reorganisation of time, student grouping and resources to support high-quality learning experiences. Schedules at Expeditionary Learning schools provide longer and more flexible blocks of time for project-based learning and fieldwork, for team planning and for community-building activities.

School Review — Expeditionary Learning schools engage in an annual cycle of reflection, planning and action to improve the quality of teaching and learning. Schools look at evidence of student work and instructional practices to assess progress toward full implementation of the 10 design principles. They set priorities for improvement, and create an action plan for achieving those priorities.

The Success: In its first 10 years, Expeditionary Learning Outward Bound has been extremely successful in transforming educational environments in the United States and Puerto Rico. In many of these schools, reading and math comprehension levels have increased, and students, parents and teachers are more engaged. More than 100 schools, 53,000 students and 3,000 teachers have been touched and inspired by this innovative form of Outward Bound.

Thompson Island Outward Bound Education Center

THOMPSON ISLAND

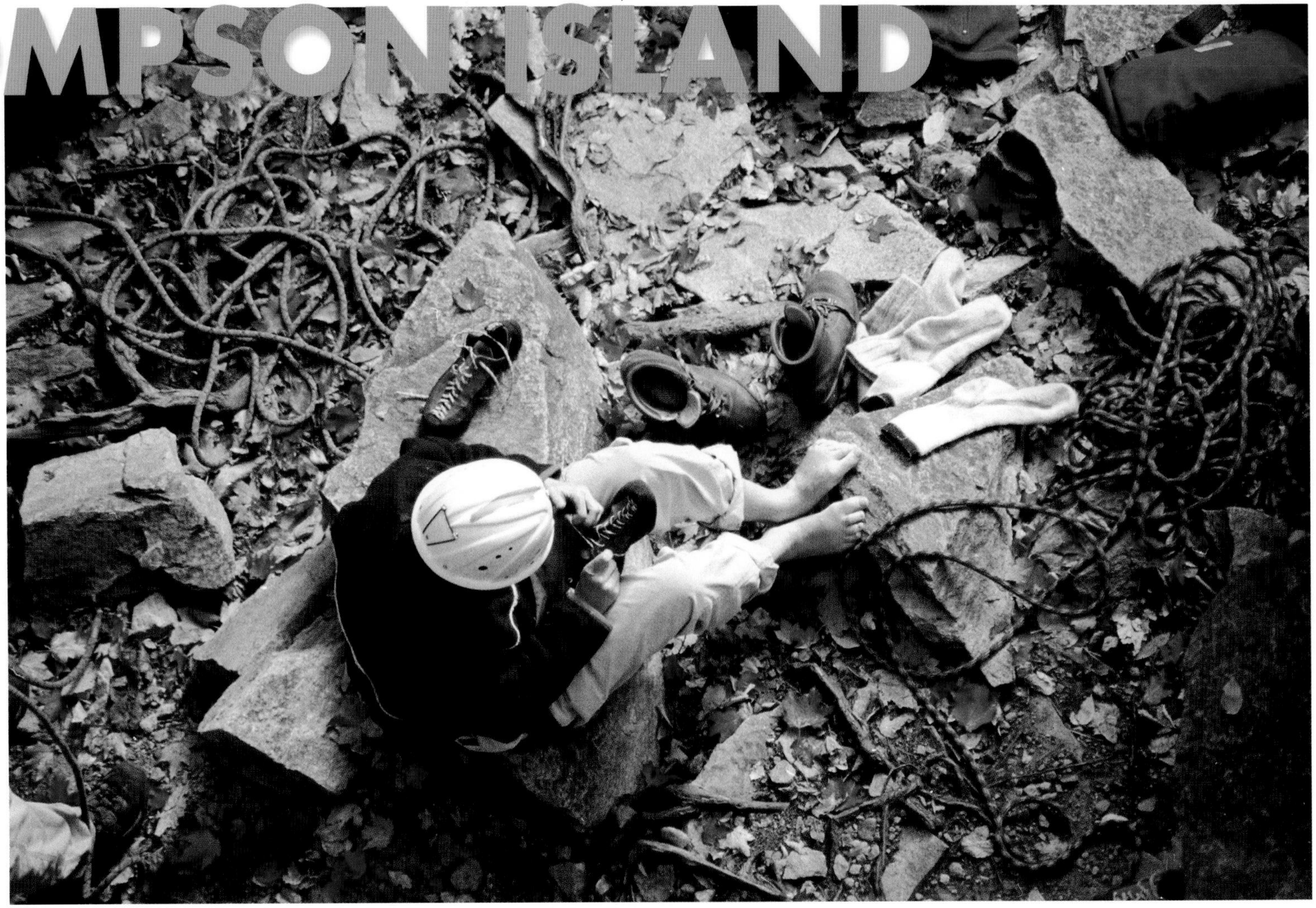

photo: Deirdra Funcheon

Located on a lush 63-hectare island in the middle of Boston Harbor, Thompson Island Outward Bound Education Center is truly an exciting place to grow for the youth of Boston. Since 1988, its programmes have reached out to urban youth during their early adolescence, a critical time of change and growth.

By connecting in challenging ways to the land, the sea and the people in their communities, students at Thompson Island Outward Bound uncover strengths in themselves and their peers. Instructor Zach See explains: "The students we serve have typically had low expectations placed on them, both in school and other aspects of their lives. Outward Bound is an extraordinary opportunity for students to prove themselves, and to show they are capable of anything."

Creating extraordinary and challenging growth opportunities is what the staff at Thompson Island do best. During the school year, they operate the only Outward Bound middle school in the world, as well as the Choices Program. This programme brings students in Boston public schools to the island for five-day expeditions involving ropes courses, camping, climbing and diversity training. In the summer, the island offers expeditions for 12 to 14 year-old girls and boys. The school also provides environmental education programmes in partnership with the New England Aquarium, long summer expeditions for at-risk youth, contract courses individually designed for schools and youth groups, and professional development programmes for corporate clients.

A woman prepares to rock-climb during a women's weekend course in Western Massachusetts, one of many adult courses that help generate revenue for the youth programmes

118

photo: Patrick Haldeman

A middle school student tests himself on Bendheim Diamond course, one of four high-challenge courses on the 82-hectare Thompson Island, which is part of the Boston Harbor Islands National Park.

photo: Deirdra Funcheon

Taking place only a short distance from downtown Boston, the Choices expedition marks the first time many urban youth have spent a night outside, cooked a meal or set foot in a national park.

photo: Deirdra Funcheon

Students live and sleep on 9-metre wooden pulling boats that can be sailed or rowed while navigating the waters of Boston Harbor and Massachusetts Bay.

"I work for Outward Bound because I want to make a difference in the lives of urban youth in particular. I see Outward Bound as a positive vehicle for change, to empower people. I'm constantly inspired by young people who make critical decisions and positive changes in their lives as result of Outward Bound."

HURRICANE ISLAND

In 1963, Peter Willauer, an experienced sailor and teacher with an immense knowledge and love for Maine's rocky coastline and offshore islands, discovered the perfect spot for the East Coast's Outward Bound school – Hurricane Island. Just off the coast of Maine, it includes an old quarry, which makes the island ideal for rock climbing and sailing activities. Today, Hurricane Island Outward Bound School is the largest in the United States. From its headquarters in Rockland, Maine, the school operates in 14 locations stretching from Maine, through Maryland and Philadelphia, all the way to the Florida Keys.

The variety of their programme offerings and expeditions is matched only by the diversity of the people who challenge themselves and participate on these courses. Participants range from teens to adults, civic organisations to school groups, and juvenile justice providers to multinational corporations. Adventures include both sea- and land-based expeditions, from pulling boat and tall-ship sailing to sea kayaking, backpacking, rock climbing and canoeing in the spring, summer and fall, and dog sledding, cross-country skiing, ice-climbing and backpacking in the winter.

The Hurricane Island Outward Bound School has inherited some of the most breathtaking wilderness in the Eastern United States. Students have countless opportunities to explore the scenic wonders of outdoor life – from the back country of the Florida Keys to the cypress-lined shores of the Suwannee River, from the Savage Wilderness of West Virginia to the estuaries of Chesapeake Bay, from the remote Northwoods of Maine to the 3,500 islands off the coast of Maine. In many cases, due to the role they play in the conservation of Maine islands, Outward Bound students have opportunities to visit places not accessible to the general public.

121

Hurricane Island Outward Bound School strives to be a beacon of light in our complex and sometimes chaotic world where confidence and self-esteem can founder. By combining the school's mission with the motto, "To serve, to strive and not to yield," staff hope to improve society by providing participants with positive experiences that can change their outlook and attitudes.

A student expresses what Hurricane Island does best: "How can people understand three weeks of not taking a shower, going to bed at 11 p.m. and getting up at 5 a.m., living and sleeping on a boat, soloing on an island for three days and three nights. How do they understand that under all these circumstances, this was the best three weeks of my life?"

A crew steers a spritsail ketch, a rugged and versatile craft, in the coastal wilderness of Penobscot Bay.

122

Casting fear aside, a student leans backwards to fall from a height into the arms of his team. This group bonding exercise is known as the "trust fall".

Abandoned by their instructor for a "ship wreck" exercise, teammates are drawn closer together while stranded overnight on a remote island.

Homeward bound from their Gulf of Mexico expedition, a crew engages relentless winds to pass beneath one of the 42 bridges that connect the Florida Keys with the U.S. mainland.

Crew members are sometimes left to solo on isolated mangrove islands of the Florida Everglades, a unique and threatened ecosystem.

"I keep my diploma from the HIOBS Maine backpacking expedition hanging in my NYC apartment. My Harvard BA and Columbia MBA diploma are in boxes in my closet. The HIOBS diploma represents the great transition period of my life – it's the one parchment I keep close. It's the one that matters."

BERMUDA

In 1970, Bermuda police officer Tony Diggins thought the youth of the country would benefit from the experience of an Outward Bound course. There had been some civil unrest in the late 1960s and a resulting inquiry recommended that the police service look at ways of fostering better relations with the youth of Bermuda. He raised enough funds, through corporate donations, to send a group to the United Kingdom for a course. This was the beginning of Outward Bound Bermuda. By 1974, the Bermuda Police Department and the Department of Youth and Sport began running Outward Bound courses in their own country, staffed entirely by police officers. A group of students still travels overseas each year – the majority of them are graduates of a local course.

Outward Bound Bermuda now offers a wide variety of programmes for youth, from one to five days in duration. By the mid 1990s, police officers began to step out of the instructor role, and civilians now operate most of the courses. Outward Bound Bermuda serves 20 percent of the youth of Bermuda and offers courses that include climbing and abseiling, high and low ropes courses, orienteering, sailing, kayaking and canoeing. The school also uses the tunnels and dungeons of a fort built in 1875 for "caving" exercises.

Over the years, Outward Bound for the Youth of Bermuda has worked closely with the Social Services Department in Bermuda to run numerous courses for youth at risk. In one programme, inmates from the youth correctional facility attend one-day courses and profit from the opportunity to earn the Duke of Edinburgh's Award while serving their time.

127

This canal, carved into solid lava, is the entrance to the mangrove-bordered Paget Island Lagoon, where students experience team-building – and the occasional mud-fight.

Precariously balancing on the barrels and planks provided, youngsters display intense concentration as they attempt to traverse a given distance without touching the ground.

After hurling himself from a tree-top platform at the centre of Paget Island, a student soars along a zip-wire and arrives at sea-level to the cheers of his fellows.

On Bermuda's eastern tip, where crews have spent hours afloat on "sunfish" boats, Fort St. Catherine looms like an apparition from centuries past.

129

Students have an opportunity to experience some of the best snorkelling in the world, such as in Tobacco Bay, with its proliferation of marine life.

COSTA RICA

Imagine... mud-soaked boots drop from your weary feet to the floor of a newly-erected tarp shelter. You sigh with relief as you sprawl onto your sleeping bag. Your mind retraces the 19 kilometres of Costa Rican rainforest you've just crossed. You smile as you recall the troop of spider monkeys that crossed your group's path earlier that day. You are utterly exhausted, but you have found perfect peace. A transformation of consciousness has occurred. Welcome to the Costa Rica Rainforest Outward Bound School (CRROBS).

CRROBS began as the dream of Jim Rowe, a former Colorado Outward Bound School instructor, who wanted to bring principle-based learning and adventure experiences into the rainforests of Costa Rica. By 1997, the Costa Rica Rainforest Outward Bound School joined the international Outward Bound community. In the process, they introduced new elements to Outward Bound, such as surfing, scuba diving, and Spanish language courses.

And there is much more — the Costa Rica Rainforest Outward Bound School's activities include waterfall rappels, rock climbs, caving, jungle trekking, white water kayaking, rafting, sea kayaking, and mountaineering. At the heart of any CRROBS course is study of the tropical environment and the native cultures of the area. Students may find themselves harvesting "frijoles" (beans) with a local mountain farmer or studying medicinal plants with an indigenous teacher. At times, the cultural lessons may be even more valuable than the experience of living in the jungle.

131

Days are long for students at CRROBS. Here, first-time surfers retreat from a scarlet ocean to make dinner and to reflect together upon the experiences of the day.

Above the forest roof, the resplendent beak of the toucan is unmistakable. The toucan is part of Costa Rica's diverse ecosystems, which support more than 1,700 species of fauna.

Natural spires of the rainforest provide an ideal venue for climbing and rappelling, with the added privilege of an upper canopy experience.

133

Students summon newly realised competence and ingenuity to undertake original methods of river crossing, far from roads or modern bridges.

Following the line of a breaking wave in search of a fish breakfast, pelicans intersect with a CRROBS surfer near Manuel Antonio, home of the best surfing in Central America.

During "homestay", students are assimilated with local families in the rainforest. After an exhausting day of challenge, a young woman seeks relief in a cascade of well-water.

In 1998, a core group of board members who had experienced Outward Bound in other parts of the world, gathered together and decided to launch Outward Bound Brazil to serve the young people of Brazil. By the year 2001, they received provisional licensing from Outward Bound International. They began operations in Chapada Diamantina, where students can trek 75 km in 12 days, and in the Serra da Mantiqueira, where students have the opportunity to climb a 2,550-metre-high peak. Both of these areas offer extraordinary backpacking with relatively easy access to major metropolitan areas.

In Chapada Diamantina, students hike for days through grasslands and dried riverbeds, stop at swimming holes, hike off-trail and perform service projects with area residents. This area is marked by a history of mining and foreign occupation. Students learn about their country's past by walking on stone-paved trails built by slaves and stopping at a remote mining settlement. The region also abounds with rivers and waterfalls, including one that is 370-metres high.

Students on three-day courses travel in self-sufficient mini-expeditions over the highlands of Serra da Mantiqueira, hiking about 20 km in altitudes ranging from 1,800 to over 2,500 metres. Highlights of the Serra da Mantiqueira include immense open views of the landscape and almost infinite route and campsite variations.

Situated in the largest South American country, with some of the richest biodiversity in the world, Outward Bound Brazil enjoys exceptional opportunities for future growth. Organisers plan to operate along the coast, in the desert, in the Amazon Rainforest and in the mountains. On all of their courses, the students learn environmental stewardship, outdoor living skills and team-building skills. Through these elements, Outward Bound Brazil provides an alternative, engaging experience for school children in Brazil.

In the heart of the state of Bahia, Brazil, lies the Chapada Diamantina. This land of rivers and high plateaus becomes temporary home for Outward Bound students on an expedition.

AUSTRALIA & NEW ZEALAND

From the windswept reaches of the Yaggerup Dunes in the west to the fertile rainforest of the north, the scope of Australian topography provides an uncommon backdrop for the Outward Bound experience.

Discover Australia! You will have a chance to, if you participate in any of the diverse course offerings at Outward Bound Australia. Since its founding in 1956, this school has made a concerted effort to operate in all the rich wilds of this vast country. Its national base is in the breathtaking Brindabella and Tidbinbilla Ranges, which are filled with a variety of wildlife, clear mountain rivers, expansive forests and spectacular rock climbing sites.

The ranges spread south and more than 4,000 km north and west from there, but mobile operations use up to 18 other operational areas as well. Programmes operate at Australia's highest mountain (Mt. Kosciuszko), the rugged mountains and temperate forests of Victoria, the tropical rainforests of Northern Queensland, the arid deserts and spectacular gorges of the Northern Territory and at the ancient Tingle and Karri Forests on the rugged headlands of Western Australia. Outward Bound Australia also administers international programmes that partner with other Outward Bound schools. Students can take courses that include caving, bush walking, ropes courses, rock climbing, abseiling, white water rafting, canoeing and more.

Outward Bound Australia has long been a leader in providing experiences that stimulate lasting personal growth. The school serves students with special needs, corporations, families, multicultural and indigenous peoples, outdoor professionals and the general public with its courses. To maintain leadership in the field of outdoor education, Outward Bound Australia has conducted extensive research on the results of its programmes, and has registered itself nationally as a training organisation for outdoor education professionals.

139

On the Northern Rivers course in New South Wales,
beginners rock climb in the last rays of daylight.

The largest of a thousand Eucalyptus varieties, this giant
Karri tree (an ideal place for abseil training) looms
30 metres above the forest floor in Western Australia.

The rainforests of Queensland become a wilderness classroom.

During mobile courses in remote wilderness areas, students often encounter fauna unique to this fascinating continent, like this joey peering from its mother's pouch.

Free-abseiling from cliffs high above the Indian Ocean, a student pauses to contemplate a remarkable view of the breathtaking coastline.

Canoeists confront white water on the Murrumbidgee River near the
Outward Bound national centre in the Australian Capital Territory.

143

Trekking the Snowy Mountains in Victoria, students develop strength and endurance
and use newly learned skills to navigate through 300 kilometres of trackless bush.

Raftsailing requires expertise and fortitude when
navigating in the gusts of Nornalup Inlet.

Students ride the river on air mattresses, their provisions tucked
beneath them, while "cascading" in Northern New South Wales.

NEW ZEALAND

Outward Bound New Zealand lies within the labyrinth of waterways of the Marlborough Sounds, where the mountains meet the sea. Located at Anakiwa, at the northeast corner of the South Island of New Zealand, the school has access to the rivers, bush, sea and nearby Rainbow Mountains, providing an ever-changing and challenging classroom in an extraordinarily beautiful environment.

Since 1962, more than 40,000 New Zealanders have experienced and benefitted from at least one Outward Bound New Zealand course. The school focuses on the transition from youth to adulthood – over 80 percent of students are between the ages of 17 and 26. Every month of the year, a group of young students sets out on a 22-day course. Shorter courses are also offered for adults, corporations and special groups, including students with physical and learning disabilities, and parents together with their teenagers.

Every step of every course at Outward Bound New Zealand is carefully designed to supplement the course purpose, objectives, curriculum and the needs of the individuals and group. Learning is relevant and transferable to everyday life. The exact content, sequence and programming of a course are generally not disclosed. This allows for surprise – encouraging resourcefulness and adaptability. Activities include sailing (and sometimes rowing!) in traditional gaff-rigged cutters, sea/river kayaking in the Marlborough Sounds, solo experiences for reflection and goal-setting, a high ropes course set in a grove of magnificent kahikatea trees, bush expeditions in beautiful native beech forest, creative-expressive activities, rock climbing/abseiling, community service and general fitness – running, swimming and aerobics.

This 10-metre cutter has alternating work stations for 14 students and is similar to the vessel used by Captain Cook to explore New Zealand in the late 1700s.

146

As an invigorating start to the day of discovery that lies ahead, an exercise
session and 3.2-kilometre run end in the dawn mist of Okiwa Bay.

An exercise to develop respect, affection and trust within a group of
strangers, a student leaps head-first into the arms of his teammates.

This new school in Bali is in the unique position to combine an Outward Bound course with an incomparable South Sea island experience. The gentle Balinese people provide a fascinating cultural experience for visiting participants.

ASIA

SRI LANKA

In 1952, a group of 16 boys between the ages of 14 and 18 began Outward Bound training at St. Thomas' College in the central hills of Sri Lanka, high up in a beautiful valley off the road that leads from Welimada to Gurutalawa. A British educator, Dr. Hayman, was principal of St. Thomas and had founded the school on the basis of Kurt Hahn's ideas.

Elderly men who were students on these first courses discuss their most compelling experiences at Outward Bound Training Sri Lanka (OBTSL), and their eyes light up. During "the expedition", each boy carried a haversack with 20 pounds of gear. This included a saucepan, a kettle, two water bottles, one spoon, one knife, one tin-cutter, two compasses, two candles, two ground sheets, one tent, two tins of corned beef, two tins of fish, two tins of condensed milk, six loaves of bread, some tea and some sugar. They were sent off with a set of coordinates on a map and were compelled to work as a group to find and reach their destination. Dr. Hayman would climb the highest mountain in the area and watch each group's progress through binoculars.

Today, OBTSL has a much different face, but its participants still leave with a gleam in their eyes and a great sense of accomplishment. At the Dambulu Oya Outward Bound Centre, professionals from companies in Sri Lanka come to test their capacity for leadership and teamwork on courses as long as seven days and as short as 12 hours. "Trainees", as they are called at OBTSL, will acquire the life skills needed to cope in a fast-moving and highly competitive work environment. Outward Bound Training Sri Lanka, in collaboration with the Sri Lanka Business Development Centre, has trained more than 2,000 executives since 1996.

Concurrently, OBTSL offers programmes for youth, embracing the natural resources of Sri Lanka – the seaside, estuaries, rivers, lakes, mountains and jungle.

Participants collect gear and begin their descent from Ritigala Rock after a long, hot afternoon of rock climbing in North Central Province.

...and "The Trust Lift".

152

Business managers turn to Outward Bound as a source of training in teamwork and leadership. Collective effort is required to successfully perform "The Trust Fall"...

Wandura monkeys seem engrossed as they observe Outward Bound activities.

153

"Build & Sail Your Raft" can be a difficult test for executives, pictured here on Habarana Lake.

BALI

Having successfully established Outward Bound Indonesia, located two hours from Jakarta, its founder, Djoko Kusumowidagdo, was inspired to extend his vision and he opened up Outward Bound Bali in early 2002. Situated deep in the rainforest on the island of Bali, the school's base camp is a three-storey building built on a steep valley slope on the Ayung River, near the internationally renowned artistic community of Ubud. As Bali is central to the eastern islands of Indonesia, the Outward Bound experience can now be opened up to the population of this region. This island is also becoming the international hub of Indonesia, making the school's open enrollment programmes accessible to people from all over the world. The friendly and peaceful Balinese society helps to make Outward Bound Bali an extremely attractive centre.

Courses began in the summer of 2002 and include team-building, high ropes, caving and various white water river activities. Students enjoy the privilege of adventuring into protected areas and lakes which are not open to the public. For example, students can hike into West Bali National Park, home to endangered species of birds and the protected Sawo Kecik trees found only here, or hike and climb in the mountains of Northern Bali, which include the famous volcano, Mount Agung. Canoeing and raftbuilding take place on the serene waters of protected lakes.

Clients range from international corporations to members of the general public to international Outward Bound students. These programmes are particularly appealing to those interested in experiencing the unique ecosystems of Bali: the rainforest, mountains, caves and the beaches and reefs of the Bali Sea.

155

An ethereal morning on a lake near one of Bali's thousands of Hindu temples seems to reflect the peaceful social climate of this beautiful island.

156

Suspended 20 metres above the wild and scenic Ayung River valley in central Bali, a young man carefully balances each step to steady the "Burma Bridge".

In deep rainforest, on the high ropes course at Outward Bound Bali's main base, students challenge themselves in new and difficult ways.

INDONESIA

"Outward Bound leads to people who never give up, who try and try again, and who reach for limits otherwise unknown." These are the words of Djoko Kusumowidagdo, founder of Outward Bound Indonesia and a man who practises what he preaches. In 1988, Djoko encountered the Outward Bound movement and immediately began pursuing an understanding of the programmes. Through consultations with Outward Bound Malaysia and Outward Bound Singapore, Djoko and his wife Elly began to realise how Outward Bound could make an enormous difference in enriching the lives of people in Indonesia.

Financing the dream was the first challenge. In the last two decades of the 20th century, Indonesia's financial situation was tenuous, which made financing Outward Bound Indonesia that much harder. Djoko had initially negotiated with a bank to sponsor Outward Bound Indonesia, but when the money was needed, the bank was on the brink of collapse. With the assistance of his father and family-owned companies, he modestly sponsored the opening of Outward Bound Indonesia in 1991. In 1998, during the Asian financial crisis, Outward Bound Indonesia once again struggled for survival with persistence and tenacity. Astonishingly, a year after the financial crisis abated, the school enjoyed a 200 percent increase in enrollment.

The second challenge was establishing a niche in Indonesian culture. Outward Bound Indonesia positioned itself as a provider of outdoor and experience-based professional development for executives, the first school of its kind in Indonesia. In the beginning, attracting professionals was difficult. But Outward Bound Indonesia set a trend, and now about a dozen companies imitate their programmes. Outward Bound Indonesia also works with people with disabilities, nuns, seminarians and youth at risk.

The third challenge was to build a strong staff and a diverse range of programmes. To ensure the highest quality of programmes, Outward Bound Indonesia brought in staff from the U.K., U.S.A., Australia and Canada. In turn, those staff trained Indonesians, who now run safe and inspiring courses out of their base camp in Jatiluhur, two hours drive from Jakarta on the island of Java. Only 150 metres from a reservoir's edge, students start their adventures in and around the water, travelling by canoe to activity sites across the lake. Programmes also include a ropes course, tracking, rafting and trekking in the surrounding mountains.

As Outward Bound Indonesia celebrated its 10th anniversary in 2001, it also celebrated its growth with the opening of a new centre in Bali.

159

Outward bound, a team hikes to meet a boat that will carry them across Lake Jatiluhur to a new world of adventure.

Rice and fish farms trace the shores of Lake Jatiluhur where students must truly dedicate themselves in order to abseil the 30-metre bluff of Batukarut.

As a communication-building exercise, group participants must rearrange the order of their positions without upsetting the fragile balance above a pool of water.

Mount Parang dominates the skyline in West Java, setting a breathtaking scene for the participants in a managerial leadership course as they propel their canoes towards base-camp at the end of the expedition on Lake Jatiluhur.

SINGAPORE

photo: OB Singapore

Outward Bound Singapore is a centre of excellence for Outward Bound training, challenging young people to achieve their potential and become better citizens.

Outward Bound Singapore has invested in building facilities and programmes that challenge and provoke learning for their participants. There are two centres: one on the island of Pulau Ubin just off the coast of Singapore, and the other, named SPARKc on the island of Singapore. These centres offer courses that range from two to 21 days in duration and reach a broad spectrum of people. The children's courses for ages 10 to 13 operate out of SPARKc; the youth and adult courses, out of Pulau Ubin. In addition, Outward Bound Singapore created the Overseas Youth Programme, which provides students from Singapore with intercultural outdoor challenge adventures at other Outward Bound centres around the world.

Nationally recognised with the Excellence in Singapore Award in the year 2000, Outward Bound Singapore has also won a Distinguished Service Award from Outward Bound International. The award acknowledged the school's assistance and leadership in the growth of Outward Bound in Southeast Asia. The Overseas Youth Programme also won the International Innovative Programming Award from Outward Bound International in 2001.

Outward Bound Singapore continues to fulfil its goals. Strong leadership, and the support of the People's Association of Singapore, ensure ongoing success, both at home and abroad.

The multi-element tower at SPARKc is a great challenge for young minds and bodies.
Located on Singapore's east coast, this training facility is designed specifically for children.

photo: OB Singapore

164

*Anticipating adventure, these participants warm
up prior to embarking on a sea expedition.*

photo: OB Singapore

*Learning through activity, students cross the thin line
between perceived limits and actualised potential.*

"In highly urbanised Singapore, to work in Outward Bound is to be presented with a rare opportunity to operate in Singapore's last remaining natural areas. The outdoors is a place where, as an Outward Bound instructor, I can introduce to participants some of its wonders."

Deep in the jungle interior of the Temburong District of Brunei lies an Outward Bound centre full of hidden splendour. To get there, one must navigate by "Temuai" (a traditional longboat) up river, trek through the tropical rainforest or helicopter down into it. Welcome to the operations centre of Outward Bound Brunei Darussalam! Only a few kilometres to the north of this centre is a slightly less remote logistics centre, from which most of the residential courses depart.

Students of Outward Bound Brunei Darussalam have the opportunity to experience first hand the challenges of living near pristine tropical wildlife sanctuaries, working in teams on white water rivers, travelling high in the canopy on challenge courses and walking above the river on an 81-metre-long suspension bridge. Because of its remoteness, the centre's electricity is derived from a generator and its water supply is obtained from the river by means of a pump and treatment plant. The centres occupy a prominent position within the lush jungle and white water terrain of Temburong. Nevertheless, continuous efforts have been made to ensure that the surrounding natural habitats are well preserved.

Nineteen-ninety-two was a historical milestone for Outward Bound Brunei Darussalam. His Majesty the Sultan of Brunei, through wisdom and vision, initiated the idea of developing an Outward Bound centre for the youth of the country. With the financial help of the Brunei Shell Petroleum Company, Shell International and the Outward Bound "know how" of Winston Lim from Outward Bound Singapore, Outward Bound Brunei Darussalam began its operations in 1997. The school now serves the citizens of Brunei with a variety of both residential and mobile courses from three to 14 days long. Staff work with local schools, colleges, universities and corporations to provide courses that encourage citizenship, responsibility and leadership.

The river coils through the heart of remote jungle carrying expeditions far from the security of the familiar to venture into the landscapes of a different world.

Courses begin with a long river journey to the logistics centre, where new groups are welcomed by staff clad in traditional Brunei raiment.

An expedition moves slowly through the tropical forest of Temburong District attempting to successfully navigate the emerald maze.

A class watches intently as an instructor demonstrates the various knots that have to be mastered before climbing.

On a river surrounded on all sides by living forest, students use inflatable kayaks to experience flat and white water challenges.

"The visit to the jungle in its beauty and freshness was a calling for the need to return to the basics of humanity. You made our experience memorable as well as valuable."

SABAH

Outward Bound Sabah, in Borneo, offers an abundance of opportunities to discover nature at its most rugged, wild and serene. It also offers a rich arena for cultural lessons. With some of the greatest ethnic diversity in the world, Sabah boasts approximately 55 major linguistic ethnic groups and more than 100 dialects.

As the sun rises over the South China Sea and Kawang River, participants begin their morning routine of exercise by running on a golden stretch of beach near the boathouse. After breakfast, cabin inspection and a briefing, students embark on their adventures. These might include sailing on Outward Bound Sabah's 8-metre whaler and then diving into the sea to explore the reef and bountiful underwater world. On expedition, students can climb Mt. Kinabalu, walk through jungles and villages, then white water raft and sea kayak to the centre or stay at the Annex in the Crocker Range.

On shorter expeditions, students learn traditional camping techniques of the interior people of Borneo by using their parang (similar to a machete) to cut wood from the jungle. The next step is to build a wood frame, tie it together with jungle vines, and place a tarpaulin over it. Students sleep communally in their "longhouse" tents and cook over traditional campfires. On the journey back to Kinarut from the jungle, they work on community service projects in small villages. On the seven-day Danum Valley expedition, students will probably see orangutans, proboscis monkeys, elephants, deer, wild boar and even rhinoceros.

Whatever the activity or location, students who participate on courses at Outward Bound Sabah are sure to experience the four pillars of Outward Bound: physical fitness, compassion for others, community service and project work designed to build team skills.

173

To experience Outward Bound is to leave behind the routine and to travel into new environments, new attitudes and new resolutions.

Clinging mist veils the Borneo jungle, where team members develop endurance

Rather than dwelling on seemingly insurmountable barriers, students are encouraged to redirect their energies into achieving positive results.

When students prove capable of maneuvering the vessel in conditions that can vary dramatically, the activity is completed without instruction.

Clinging mist veils the Borneo jungle where team members develop endurance and interdependence during the adventure of an expedition.

LUMUT

Malaysia's Outward Bound School in Lumut has a proud history. It was one of the first centres established outside the United Kingdom.

In 1952, a member of the Outward Bound Trust of the UK visited what was then Malaya in the hopes of founding a sea school, like the Outward Bound School in Aberdovey. The sea school was to offer to Malayan industry, the educational establishment, youth organisations, trade unions, the government and public authorities, parents and others the opportunity to provide special character training for their young men. This idea became a reality in 1955, when the first courses began.

Outward Bound Lumut, set on the western coast of peninsular Malaysia, is surrounded by the islands of Pangkor and Pulau Sembilan and features rainforests and mountains. The school offers courses from three to 25 days that include either a sea expedition (by whaler, kayak or raft) or a land expedition (solo camping, rock climbing, rappelling, orienteering, trekking and rope course activities). The popularity of these classic courses remains high, a testament to the original vision of Outward Bound.

From its beginning, this school has sought to design programmes that support and inspire good communications within the Malaysian multi-racial society of Malays, Chinese, Indians, Eurasians and Europeans. They are also able to reach out to younger children with shorter courses that fit children's developmental needs. Outward Bound Lumut's current vision is to create situations and opportunities to learn, to share and to develop people's capacities in order to build a brighter tomorrow.

With map and compass to navigate the dense jungle of Western Malaysia, team members hope to use newly acquired skills to reach the chosen campsite before nightfall.

Having experienced the personal drama that has left so many graduates with a sense of tremendous fulfillment, students savour the last night of their course.

A splash of crimson against the island of Pangkor, a sailing expedition puts to sea in Western Malaysia.

Fortifying his bivouac with coconut fronds, a 10-year-old boy begins his solo adventure.

THAILAND

In 2000, Outward Bound Thailand opened its doors for its first courses. One course was designed for a scholarship group of 20 under-privileged youth from the Human Development Centre in Bangkok, and the other for eight officials from the Ministry of Education. Since then, Outward Bound Thailand has also served leading corporations by providing professional and team development courses.

The school seeks to make a significant impact on the lives of Thai youth, while also introducing experiential education, action learning and environmental conservation to Thailand. To serve this vision, Outward Bound Thailand has set up a foundation to provide funding for outdoor industry professional training and community environmental projects. In one course for national park rangers, Outward Bound Thailand staff were able to teach the wilderness skills that rangers need to track the disappearing Asian tiger and to fight off poachers.

Outward Bound Thailand operates six- to 21-day courses for youth ages 16 and up. It also offers one- to five-day customised corporate team-building or professional development programmes. Most of these programmes start at the school base at the mouth of the Pranburi River, just 20 kilometres south of Hua Hin in the Gulf of Thailand, and less than three hours drive from Bangkok. Hua Hin and Pranburi are within reach of spectacular natural parks such as the Kaeng Krachang National Park and Khao Sam Roi Yod National Park.

The school has residential, catering and dining facilities for up to 100 participants at any one time. Outward Bound Thailand has also developed courses for clients off-base in other areas of Thailand including the resort islands. The school's scope of activities includes land, river and sea expeditions that offer jungle trekking, camping, kayaking, orienteering, caving, rock climbing, abseiling, raft building and team problem-solving.

Outward Bound programmes are not easy and are not meant to be. They are designed so that everyone can succeed at their own level — all that is required is the willingness to try.

Midway through their hike from beach, through jungle and up jagged limestone peaks, a corporate group pauses to take in the spectacular view from a well-earned vantage point.

Improving their ability to tackle a problem as a team, managers participate in team dynamics at school base in Hua Hin.

183

Hikers in the rainforest of Khao Sam Roi Yod National Park encounter a labyrinth of roots and vines.

HONG KONG

As the mist lifts over Tai Mong Tsai, the headquarters of Outward Bound Hong Kong, outlines of peaks, glittering coastline filled with sea caves and stunning beaches appear. On any given day at Outward Bound Hong Kong, you can see youth and adults of all walks of life challenging themselves as they learn to navigate the waters in kayaks and sailboats. You may also see students taking risks on the high ropes events, struggling to climb up a rock or mountain, and pushing each other to build the best, most effective raft to set out onto the water.

Outward Bound Hong Kong has a rich tradition of integrating personal growth and development with group leadership and teamwork. One recent 24-year old graduate describes this integration well: "This was a rewarding journey of discovery. I discovered the beauty of nature, the power and enjoyment of teamwork, the skills of problem-solving, true friendship, my own strengths and weaknesses, proper attitudes towards other people and my potential."

Adventures at Outward Bound Hong Kong range from five- to 15-days long. Courses at Tai Mong Tsai have incorporated a wide range of training facilities. At the more remote centre, Wong Wan Chau Adventure Base, participants can catch a glimpse of the wild beauty, peace and tranquillity of the southern end of Double Haven in Mirs Bay. Every year, Outward Bound Hong Kong organises international adult expeditions to places such as Malaysia, the Philippines, Japan, Nepal, Europe and North America.

185

Following initial work in 1995, Outward Bound Hong Kong founded a new Outward Bound school in China in 1998. Outward Bound Hong Kong is now working to develop this into a fully self-reliant operation.

Sea kayakers ride undulating swells amidst beautiful, cave-pocked islands in the sheltered waters off Hong Kong's inner harbour.

For a group overlooking the pastoral serenity of Tai Mong Tsai, it's hard to believe that the bustling city of Hong Kong is only a few kilometres away.

Crews make voyages of two to three days on ketch-rigged cutters like the "Fay Fung" (Flying Wind) shown here

"My heart was full of satisfaction, in sharp contrast to the exhaustion I felt throughout my body. Hot, uncontrollable tears were streaming down my cheeks. It was only a 20-metre climb, but I had learned many things from this experience – fear of death, challenge, spirit, trust, my own power, camaraderie, achievement. So this is what Outward Bound is all about!" (Outward Bound Japan student)

Giving the youth of Japan this type of adventure and learning is what Koichi Inasawa sought to do when, in 1974, he conceived Outward Bound Japan. It took 15 years to fully realise that dream. By 2000, Outward Bound Japan had touched the lives of more than 14,000 students.

Outward Bound Japan's national base is located in Otari, a small village in the northernmost part of Nagano Prefecture. Out of Otari, students can glimpse part of ancient history as they walk the legendary Salt Road. East of Otari is Mt. Amakazari, a lone, cone-shaped peak that rises 1,963 metres above sea level. On a clear day, a 360-degree view of the Japan Sea, Sado Island, the Noto Peninsula and the peaks of the North Alps can be seen from the mountain tops around Otari.

Students at Outward Bound Japan can participate in a variety of activities suited to ages eight and up. These activities include mountaineering, trekking, ski touring, kayaking, rafting, mountain biking, rock climbing and waterfall rock climbing. Courses range from a three- to five-day discovery programme to a 21-day traverse of Japan, to a 75-day outdoor instructor training programme.

Self-discovery is the common theme that runs through all the programmes. Perhaps the words of Koichi Inasawa capture best what Outward Bound Japan does for the youth of Japan: "With all the excitement over new high-tech innovations, computer wizardry and so on, it's easy to forget that the biggest challenge we face is not advancing the abilities of machines around us, but in advancing ourselves — in particular, giving our youth the skills and attitudes they need to function as effective and caring adults."

Outward Bound programmes offer a chance to leave behind the safe harbours of family and routine to face life-changing challenges that are uncomfortable, difficult and certainly adventure-filled.

190

Assembled on the deep, icy waters of Lake Aoki, participants practise kayak capsise and self-rescue drills before facing white water rapids.

Rugged mountains surrounding the Nagano school offer superb climbing opportunities for Japanese students.

Sawanobori is an ancient method of stream climbing by which team members rely on each other to scale slippery rocks and even waterfalls.

Sawanobori is an ancient method of stream climbing by which team members rely on each other to scale slippery rocks and even waterfalls.

Clouds "dance" on the slopes of Mount Hakuba — a breathtaking setting for this group on its final expedition. From Outward Bound, they will return with the gifts of self-esteem and confidence, and the knowledge that they have been on a rare adventure.

"At the end of the course, I could feel a great power, but this was not a new power. I had discovered a great power which already existed inside of me. Now I know that I can use this new-found power to make more and more progress in my life."

International Office

Outward Bound International
1639 East Trevino Rd., Sandy
Salt Lake City, UT 84092-5846
USA
Bus: 1 (801) 673-7345
Bus Fax: 1(775) 249-9766
E-mail: obinternational@globalserve.net
Web Page: www.outward-bound.org

Affiliate members

Australia

Outward Bound Australia
National Base, Naas Road
Tharwa, ACT 2620
Australia
Bus: 61 (2) 62 375158
Bus 2: 1 (800) 267999 (within Australia)
Bus Fax: 61 (2) 62375224
E-mail: info@outwardbound.com.au
Web Page: www.outwardbound.com.au

Belgium

Outward Bound Belgie
Kapucijnenvoer 217
3000 Leuven
Belgium
Bus: 32 16235172
Bus Fax: 32 16290309
E-mail: info@outwardbound.be
Web Page: www.outwardbound.be

Bermuda

Outward Bound for the Youth of Bermuda
Police Headquarters, P.O. Box HM 530
Hamilton HM CX
Bermuda
Bus: 1 (441) 295-0011 ext. 257
Bus Fax: 1 (441) 299-4459
E-mail: outbound@ibl.bm
Web Page: www.outwardboundbermuda.free.bm

Brazil**

Outward Bound Brasil
Rua Carmo do Rio Verde, 241 - 9 andar
04729-010 SÜo Paulo -, SP
Brazil
Bus: 55 (11) 5641-4124.
Bus Fax: 55 (11) 5641-4028
E-mail: contato@obb.org.br
Web Page: www.obb.org.br

Brunei

Outward Bound Brunei Darussalam
Ministry of Culture,Youth and Sports
Simpang 336 Jalan Kebangsaan
Bandar Seri Begawan BS4415
Brunei Darussalam
Bus: 673 (2) 382970
Bus 2: 673 (2) 382971
Bus Fax: 673 (2) 382972
E-mail: OBBD@brunet.bn
Web Page: www.kkbs.gov.bn/program.htm

Bulgaria

Outward Bound Bulgaria
Knjaz Boris I, 65B
1000 Sofia
Bulgaria
Bus: 359 (2) 981 47 09
Bus 2: 359 (2) 981 42 65
Bus Fax: 359 (2) 981 42 65
E-mail: kpavlova@outwardbound-bg.org
E-mail 2: ob@mbox.cit.bg
Web Page: www.outwardbound-bg.org

Canada

Outward Bound Canada
996 Chetwynd Rd., RR#2
Burk's Falls, ON P0A 1C0
Canada
Bus: 1 (705) 382-5454
Bus 2: 1 (888) OUTWARD (688-9273)
Bus Fax: 1 (705) 382-5959
E-mail: info@outwardbound.ca
Web Page: www.outwardbound.ca

Costa Rica

Costa Rica Rainforest Outward Bound School
P.O. Box 243
Quepos
Costa Rica
Bus: 506 777 1222
Bus Fax: 506 777 0052
E-mail: info@crrobs.org
Web Page: www.crrobs.org

Czech Republic

Outward Bound Czech Way Ceska cesta
Senovazne namesti 24
116 47 Prague 1
Czech Republic
Bus: 420 (2) 24102 334
Bus 2: 420 (2) 24102 234
Bus Fax: 420 (2) 24 102 233
E-mail: jarmila.outratova@ceskacesta.cz
Web Page: www.outwardbound.cz

Finland

Outward Bound Finland
Askonkatu 5
15100 Lahti
Finland
Bus: 358 (3) 751 66 42
Mobile: 358 (40) 5050 355
Bus Fax: 358 (3) 751 66 42
E-mail: toimisto@outwardbound.fi
Web Page: www.outwardbound.fi

Germany

Outward Bound Germany
Deutsche Gesellschaft für EuropSische Erziehung
e.V.
Nymphenburgerstr. 42
D-80335 MÜnchen
Germany
Bus: 49 (89) 121 511 0
Bus Fax: 49 (89) 121 511 10
E-mail: ob@outwardbound.de
Web Page: www.outwardbound.de

Hong Kong

Outward Bound Hong Kong
Tai Mong Tsai
Sai Kung, New Territories
Hong Kong
Bus: 852 2792 4333
Bus Fax: 852 27929877
E-mail: adoff@outwardbound.org.hk
Web Page: www.outwardbound.org.hk

Outward Bound China
5/F No. 1 Plant Building
Guangzhou Scienetech Park
North-side Chuang Ye Rd., GETDD
Guangzhou 510730
China
Bus: 86 (20) 82217296
Bus Fax: 86 (20) 82217283
E-mail: chinamarket@outwardboundchina.org
E-mail 2: chinamarket@outwardboundhk.org
Web Page: www.outwardboundchina.org

Hungary

Outward Bound Magyarorszàg Trust
H-1015 Budapest
Batthyany St. 31, 2nd Floor
Hungary
Bus: 36 12128491
Mobile: 36 209532225
Bus Fax: 36 12128491
E-mail: office@outwardbound.hu
Web Page: www.outwardbound.hu

Indonesia

Outward Bound Indonesia
Jalan Kemanggisan Utama III/14
Jakarta 11480
Indonesia
Bus: 62 (21) 548 1529
Bus 2: 62 (21) 536 0932
Bus Fax: 62 (21) 532 2546
E-mail : obindo@cbn.net.id
Web Page: www.outwardboundindo.com

Outward Bound Bali
Kompleks Segitiga Emas No. 22
Simpang Siur
Jl. By Pass I Gusti Ngurah Rai
Kuta, Bali 80361
Indonesia
Ph: (361) 75-85-99
Fax: (361) 75-86-99
Email: OBBali@yahoo.com
Web page: www.OBBali.com

Japan

Outward Bound Japan
Rm 422 Sanno Grand Building
14-2, Negata-cho 2-Chome
Chiyoda-ku
Tokyo 100
Japan
Bus: 81 335803451
Bus Fax: 81 335813633
E-mail: obsjapan@feis.com
Web Page: www.feis.com/obs

Kenya

Outward Bound Trust of Kenya
P.O. Box 49576
Kenya Cultural Centre
Nairobi
Kenya
Bus: 254 (222) 8764
Bus Fax: 254 (225) 1784
E-mail: obtkenya@onlinekenya.com

The Republic of Korea**

Outward Bound Exploratory Committee Korea
C/o nexFree
3F. Poong-LimB/D
Yoksam-dong
Kangam-gu
Seoul
Korea 135-784
Bus: 8 2 2 753 8004
Email: hkyoo@nexfree.com
Bus: 82 2 561 7310
Email: holydiver@nexfree.com

Malaysia

Outward Bound Lumut
Teluk Batik
32200 Lumut, Perak
Malaysia
Bus: 60 56835077
Bus Fax: 60 56835933
E-mail: info@obslumut.org
Web Page: www.obslumut.org

Outward Bound Sabah
Locked Bag 181
88745 Kota Kinabalu, Sabah
East Malaysia
Bus: 60 88750311
Bus Fax: 60 88750312
E-mail: obsabah@outward.po.my
Web Page:
www.infosabah.com.my/outwardbound

New Zealand

Outward Bound Trust of New Zealand
P.O. Box 3158
Wellington
New Zealand
Bus: 64 (4) 4723440
Bus Fax: 64 (4) 4728059
E-mail: info@outwardbound.co.nz
Web Page: www.outwardbound.co.nz

Romania

Outward Bound Romania Trust for Youth
RO-4300 Targu-Mures
55 Piata Trandafirilor
Romania
Bus: 40 (65) 210 905
Bus Fax: 40 (65) 210 905
E-mail: office@outwardbound.ro
Web Page: www.outwardbound.ro

Singapore

Outward Bound Singapore
c/o People's Association
9 Stadium Link
397750
Singapore
Bus: 65 (540) 0127
Bus Fax: 65 (545) 8849
E-mail: OBS_PROG@pa.gov.sg
Web Page: www.obs.org.sg

Slovak Republic

Outward Bound Slovak Republic
Studio Zazitku
Cervenova 4, 811 03 Bratislava
Slovak Republic
Bus: 421-7-544 18 073
Bus Fax: 421-7-544 14 130
E-mail: tamara@euroweb.sk
Web Page: www.outwardbound.sk

South Africa

Outward Bound Trust of South Africa
Box 3586
Knysna
South Africa
Bus: +27 44 382 7412
Bus Fax: 27 (44) 3827417
E-mail: obt.mk@mweb.co.za
Web Page: www.outwardbound.co.za

Sri Lanka

Outward Bound Trust of Sri Lanka
P.O. Box No. 2096
03 Colombo
Sri Lanka
Bus: (94 1) 434952
Bus 2: (94 1) 437684-5.
Bus Fax: 94 (1) 541170
E-mail: jcratwat@sri.lanka.net
Web Page: www.lanka.net/obsl/

Switzerland*

Outward Bound Schweiz
Gerbehof
CH- 3465 Dürrenroth
Bus: +41-878-880021
Bus Fax: +41-878-880020
E-mail: info@outwardbound.ch
Web Page: www.outwardbound.ch

Thailand

Outward Bound Thailand
6th Fl., Green Tower
3656/65 Rama 4 Rd
Klongtoey
Bangkok 10110
Thailand
Bus: 66 (2) 240 0016
Bus 2: 66 (02) 2493275
Bus Fax: 66 (2) 240 0017
E-mail: info@outwardboundthailand.org
Web Page: www.outwardboundthailand.org

United Kingdom

Outward Bound UK Trust
207 Waterloo Road
London
SE1 8XD
United Kingdom
Bus: 44 0870 5134227
Bus Fax: 44 (207) 928 3733
E-mail: enquiries@outwardbound-uk.org
Web Page: www.outwardbound-uk.org

United States of America

Outward Bound USA National
100 Mystery Point Road
Garrison, NY 10524-9757
Bus: 1 (888) 88Bound
Bus 2: 1 (845) 424-4000
Bus Fax: 1 (845) 424-4280
E-mail: info@obusa.org
Web Page: www.outwardbound.org

Colorado Outward Bound School
910 Jackson St.
Golden, CO 80401
Bus: 1 (866) 746-9777
Bus 2: 1 (800) 477-2627
Bus 3: 1 (720) 497-2400
Bus Fax: 1 (720) 497-2401
E-mail: info@cobs.org
Web Page: www.cobs.org

Expeditionary Learning Outward Bound
100 Mystery Point Road
Garrison, NY 10524-9757
Bus: 1 (845) 424-4000
Bus Fax: 1 (845) 424-4280
E-mail: farrell@elob.org
Web Page: www.elob.org

196

Hurricane Island Outward Bound School
75 Mechanic Street
Rockland, ME 04841
Bus: 1 (207) 594-5548
Bus 2: 1 (866) 746 9771
Bus Fax: 1 (207) 594-9425
E-mail: info@hurricaneisland.org
Web Page: www.hurricaneisland.org

North Carolina Outward Bound School
2582 Riceville Road
Ashville, NC 28805
Bus: 1 (828) 299-3366
Bus 2: 1 (800) 841-0186
Bus Fax: 1 (828) 299-3928
E-mail: info@ncobs.org
Web Page: www.ncobs.org
New York City Outward Bound Center
29-46 Northern Boulevard
Long Island City, NY 11101
Bus: 1 (718) 706-9900
Bus Fax: 1 (718) 433-0500
E-mail: info@nycoutwardbound.org
Web Page: www.nycoutwardbound.org

Pacific Crest Outward Bound School
0110 SW Bancroft Street
Portland, OR 97201
Bus: 1 (503) 243-1993
Bus Fax: 1 (503) 274-7723
E-mail: Craigtrames@pcobs.org
Web Page: www.pcobs.org

Thompson Island Outward Bound
Education Center
P.O. Box 127
Boston, MA 02127
Bus: 1 (617) 328-3900
Bus Fax: 1 (617) 328-3710
E-mail: info@thompsonisland.org
Web Page: www.thompsonisland.org

Voyageur Outward Bound School
101 East Chapman Street
Ely, MN 55731
Bus: 1 (800) 321- hike
Bus 2: 1 (218) 365-7790
Bus Fax: 1 (218) 365-7076
E-mail: vobs@vobs.com
Web Page: www.vobs.org

Zimbabwe
Outward Bound Zimbabwe
Chimanimani Centre, P.O. Box 57
Chimanimani
Zimbabwe
Bus: 263 (26) 2935
Bus 2: 263 (26) 2936
Bus Fax: 263 (26) 2937
E-mail: outward@internet.co.zw

197

* denotes Exploratory License
** denotes Provisional License

Creative Team Biographies

Deanna Bean

Deanna Bean, born in London, England, came to Canada in 1963 and resides in Burlington, Ontario. As a businesswoman, she has worked in communications and marketing for more than 20 years. In addition, she has contributed as a writer, researcher and/or photographer to the following publications: "Holy Grail Across the Atlantic: The Secret History of Canadian Discovery and Exploration," "More than a Myth: The Search for the Monster of Muskrat Lake," and "Greater Hamilton from the Heart." Email address: dbean@interlog.com

Rebecca Bear

Rebecca has been working in outdoor education for over 12 years. She has worked in the field for Outward Bound at the Pacific Crest School, Thompson Island Outward Bound Education Center, and in a start up operation in Mexico. At these schools she has served as an instructor, course director, staff trainer and general operations manager. Currently, Rebecca works as Program Consultant for Outward Bound International (OBI). One of the many hats Rebecca wears at OBI is editor of communications including a quarterly newsletter, electronic newsletter, website and marketing materials. Rebecca has also been a leader in organizing conferences in the United States on Women's Outdoor Leadership. She has a Master of Education Degree from Harvard University and a Bachelor's degree in American Studies from Reed College. She lives in Seattle, Washington, USA.

Craig Ketchen

Initially trained in photography at Sheridan College in Oakville, Ontario, Canada, and working in the advertising photography industry for 8 years, Craig made the transition to graphic design in 1993. Over the last 9 years, Craig has done work for such international clients as Sony, Pioneer, Panasonic, Stanley Tools, Raleigh, KitchenAid, and Whirlpool as well as many regional clients. Craig's design approach is one of a clean, detail-oriented, corporate discipline. You can visit Craig's website at www.pillar.cx.

Acknowledgements

I am thankful to Deanna Bean for editing the text, and for gracing this project with her intelligence, courage and friendship. Her contribution to this work is vast.

To Rebecca Bear, who embraced the daunting task of writing the Outward Bound school profiles — thank you for working with such tenacity throughout this project.

I am grateful to Craig Ketchen for his hard work and patience, from proposal design to final layout.

This book would probably not exist without the generous contribution of time and expertise from Jane George, Andrew Nigel and Cesar Teves. My thanks go to Benjamin Koo and Alden Li at Book Art Inc. for helping me bring another book to fruition.

I would like to extend my appreciation to all of the sponsors, with special thanks to Yunus Kara, Tom Bochsler, Joan Henderson, Dave Foxcroft, Norm Sutherland, and to Ron Beck and Noreen Calderbank, the original sponsors of The Inward Odyssey Volume I. For their contribution to Volume I, my thanks go to Doreen Gregson and Michael Waldin.

To all the Outward Bound staff who guided me through the wilderness, thank you. For their kind support of this project, I am particularly grateful to Ian Wade, Ruby Best, Derek Pritchard (OBI), Rudy Massimo, Deborah Freeman, Spencer Higdon and Bob Henderson (Canada), Deirdra Funcheon (Thompson Island, U.S.A.), Mark Norman and family (Bermuda), Yves Verraes (Belgium), Adam Horvath and family (Romania), all at OB Czech Republic, Alex Mzunza (Kenya), Djoko and Elly Kusumowidagdo (Bali), Keith Choules (Hong Kong), Koichi Inasawa (Japan), Mohammad bin Dollah (Brunei), Hayati Suaidi (Singapore) and to Charles Costello III, and Liz Cunningham of Kurt Hahn.org.

Special thanks to my travel agent Helen Britt, and to Paul Sweeney, Morris Mercanti, Robert Bagliolid, Franco Loparco, Andy Luukkonen, Peter Mercanti, Mike Grybko, David Bibby, Branislav Ristic, Tharme Design, Jerry Hordichuk, Linda Mackenzie, Val Attanasio, Larry Russell, Hamilton Mayor Bob Wade, Kelley Horton and Helen Thorpe.

I would like to thank my mother, Loraine, my brother Jon for standing by me, brother Matt for taking care of dad, and Iza and Claudia for your advice, support and love.

Thanks to God for all good things.

In memory of Joseph Zelinski, John Greene, Kevin Ewart and Josh Miner.